I0414325

Editor-in-Chief and Founder:
   Lyndon H. LaRouche, Jr.
Editorial Board: *Lyndon H. LaRouche, Jr. , Helga Zepp-LaRouche, Robert Ingraham, Tony Papert, Gerald Rose, Dennis Small, Jeffrey Steinberg, William Wertz*
Co-Editors: *Robert Ingraham, Tony Papert*
Managing Editor: *Nancy Spannaus*
Technology: *Marsha Freeman*
Books: *Katherine Notley*
Ebooks: *Richard Burden*
Graphics: *Alan Yue*
Photos: *Stuart Lewis*
Circulation Manager: *Stanley Ezrol*

INTELLIGENCE DIRECTORS
Counterintelligence: *Jeffrey Steinberg, Michele Steinberg*
Economics: *John Hoefle, Marcia Merry Baker, Paul Gallagher*
History: *Anton Chaitkin*
Ibero-America: *Dennis Small*
Russia and Eastern Europe: *Rachel Douglas*
United States: *Debra Freeman*

INTERNATIONAL BUREAUS
Bogotá: *Miriam Redondo*
Berlin: *Rainer Apel*
Copenhagen: *Tom Gillesberg*
Houston: *Harley Schlanger*
Lima: *Sara Madueño*
Melbourne: *Robert Barwick*
Mexico City: *Gerardo Castilleja Chávez*
New Delhi: *Ramtanu Maitra*
Paris: *Christine Bierre*
Stockholm: *Ulf Sandmark*
United Nations, N.Y.C.: *Leni Rubinstein*
Washington, D.C.: *William Jones*
Wiesbaden: *Göran Haglund*

ON THE WEB
e-mail: eirns@larouchepub.com
www.larouchepub.com
www.executiveintelligencereview.com
www.larouchepub.com/eiw
Webmaster: *John Sigerson*
Assistant Webmaster: *George Hollis*
Editor, Arabic-language edition: *Hussein Askary*

EIR (ISSN 0273-6314) *is published weekly (50 issues), by EIR News Service, Inc., P.O. Box 17390, Washington, D.C. 20041-0390. (703) 297-8434*

European Headquarters: E.I.R. GmbH, Postfach Bahnstrasse 9a, D-65205, Wiesbaden, Germany
Tel: 49-611-73650
Homepage: http://www.eir.de
e-mail: info@eir.de
Director: Georg Neudecker

Montreal, Canada: 514-461-1557
eir@eircanada.ca

Denmark: EIR - Danmark, Sankt Knuds Vej 11, basement left, DK-1903 Frederiksberg, Denmark.
Tel.: +45 35 43 60 40, Fax: +45 35 43 87 57. e-mail: eirdk@hotmail.com.

Mexico City: EIR, Sor Juana Inés de la Cruz 242-2 Col. Agricultura C.P. 11360
Delegación M. Hidalgo, México D.F.
Tel. (5525) 5318-2301
eirmexico@gmail.com

Canada Post Publication Sales Agreement #40683579

Postmaster: Send all address changes to *EIR*, P.O. Box 17390, Washington, D.C. 20041-0390.

Signed articles in *EIR* represent the views of the authors, and not necessarily those of the Editorial Board.

New York City in the World Land-Bridge

EIRContents

www.larouchepub.com Volume 44, Number 22, June 2, 2017

**Cover
This Week**

*Manhattan,
looking south.*

public domain

I. Helga Zepp-LaRouche in China

ONLY A BYSTANDER?

Once the United States Joins the Belt and Road Initiative, a New Paradigm for Mankind Can Begin

by Helga Zepp-LaRouche, Founder and President of the German Schiller Institute

May 29—China Investment Magazine, supervised by China's National Development and Reform Commission, carried this article by Helga Zepp-LaRouche in its May issue. The article was distributed both in Chinese and in English to every participant in the May 14-15 Belt and Road Forum for International Cooperation in Beijing. The article has been edited.

While initially almost all U.S. think-tanks were negative concerning China's Belt and Road Initiative (BRI), or simply refused even to take note of it, there has recently been a shift. Except for the hardcore neocon think-tanks, several now have started to report on the tremendous business opportunities the New Silk Road project would offer to U.S. enterprises. This has been especially true since the very successful summit, despite difficult circumstances, between President Xi Jinping and President Trump in Mar-a-Lago, Florida.

The most obvious of many areas of such cooperation would of course be the link between the Belt and Road Initiative and the planned $1 trillion infrastructure investment President Trump promised in his election campaign, which is supposed to be presented in May. There are several roadblocks to be overcome for this to happen.

The infrastructure requirements of the United States are enormous, due to decades-long non-investment by the previous administrations. Except for those who have actually been to China, most Americans have no idea how far behind China is U.S. infrastructural develop-

Beijing-Shanghai High-Speed Railway, shown in Beijing.

Wikipedia

A large Amtrak and Metro coach yard in Chicago, IL. About 25 percent of all rail traffic in the United States travels through the Chicago area.

ment is. The average speed of the Washington-Boston 736 km Acela "high-speed" line is only 105 km/h, with only very short segments at 145 km/h. This is by no means high speed, compared to the approximately 130,000 kilometers of high-speed rail in China, which amounts to over 50 times as much! U.S. roads are in terribly dangerous condition, and so are the bridges, and sanitation systems—but their use is still expensive. For a trip between Washington and New York, one has to pay the substantial amount of $115 in tolls and gas per car.

The American Society of Civil Engineers, at a recent conference, released the estimate that current U.S. infrastructure investment requirements are actually $4.5 trillion. There is no way that the financing of either of these amounts will come from the private equity market. Representatives of this sector in recent discussions with President Trump, put forward prohibitive conditions, such as an 11-12% return per annum, and a full return of the capital invested within ten years. The idea that the infrastructure should be financed by a toll system is also problematic. Even if that might barely work in some densely populated areas, it would certainly fail in thinly inhabited areas. But the very idea that there should be an immediate direct return on infrastructure investment, shows complete ignorance of the role infrastructure plays in the general economy.

The quality and density of infrastructure is a necessary precondition for the productivity of an economy as a whole. A modern economy requires that approximately 50% of its total expenditures should be designated to be used for the expansion and modernization of infrastructure, since the life expectancy of infrastructure's various categories is between 20 and 50 years. A well planned infrastructure platform is an integrated system of high-speed rail lines, waterways, highways, energy production and distribution, and communications, as well as so-called soft infrastructure such as health and education systems. The higher the technological development and productivity of an economic space becomes, the more important the speed and efficiency of the transport and density of infrastructure in general will need to be, since all the various levels of production into semi-finished and finished goods work together like a complicated machine, where each part has a role for a harmonious function.

Thus, the return on infrastructure investment is actually measured by the increase of the productivity of the entire economy. Therefore the financing can not be left to the private investor, but it must be the responsibility of the state, which is devoted to the common good of the national economy.

The Potential of U.S.-China Cooperation

If President Trump were to simply request of Congress that it fund the infrastructure program through the Federal budget, he would run into the same opposition from the Democrats and part of the GOP that has already prevented the repeal of Obamacare. And if China and other foreign investors were simply to invest by means of the private equity market—provided that were allowed—these investments would potentially be exposed to the fluctuations of the markets.

Because of decades-long policies of outsourcing to cheap labor countries, the U.S. manufacturing sector presently lacks a complete upstream and downstream industry chain, which is another impediment. China, on the other hand, has such a complete upstream and

Xinhua

China Roads and Bridges Corporation demonstrates new technology for laying track at the standard gauge railway project in Kenya, Oct. 29, 2015.

downstream industry chain, and it also has vast experience in the building of modern infrastructure systems, not only from its experience in China itself, but also from having built such systems in other countries.

China could therefore not only help those cities with the greatest transportation needs, such as New York, Los Angeles, Boston, Chicago, San Francisco, and Washington, D.C., but it could also help to replicate what China is doing domestically, namely connecting all major cities with high-speed rail systems.

For regions like the one between New York, New Jersey, and Philadelphia, for example, an integrated infrastructure system like the system planned for "Integrated Transport Development" of the Beijing-Tianjin-Hebei region, would make a lot of sense, since people are losing many hours every day commuting back and forth between their living quarters and work. While it takes only five hours to travel the distance of 800 miles from Beijing to Shanghai at an average speed of 185 mph (298 km/h), it takes 19 hours from New York City to Chicago, about the same distance!

The United States would also ben-

efit greatly from the construction of entirely new cities, which could be located in the very thinly populated areas in the central states of the United States They could be science cities, such as education and research centers, or they could be located near other, much needed large infrastructure projects, such as water management projects for the drought-endangered regions of the Southwest. One such project, which has been on the shelf since the Kennedy Administration, is the North American Water and Power Alliance, NAWAPA, which has recently been upgraded for the 21st Century.

On the other hand, such an upgraded U.S. economy could also export into the expanding Chinese market. The Chinese middle class—of approximately 900 million people—is enjoying a rapidly increasing buying power, made possible by the structural reforms implemented by the Chinese government. In 2016, the bilateral trade volume between the United States and China was already $519.6 billion, and bilateral investment grew to $170 billion in the same year. Over the last decade, U.S. exports to China grew 11%, and Chinese investments in the United States grew 5.6%. The growth potential for all of these categories is enormous,

Xinhua/Liang Xu

Photo taken on July 31, 2015 shows the last 500 meters of ballastless track of Foshan-Zhaoqing intercity rail line, in south China's Guangdong Province.

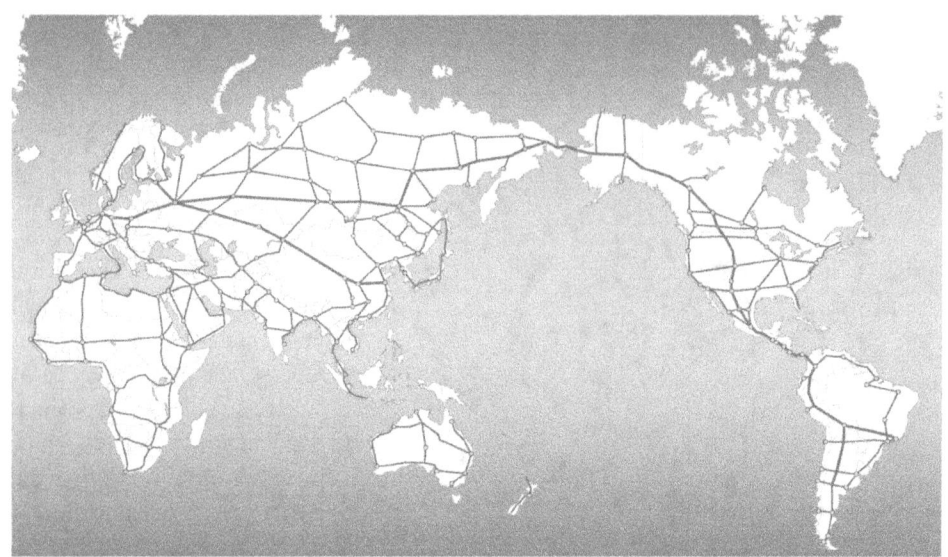

A diagram of the proposed World Land-Bridge reaching from the southern tip of South America in Chile and Argentina, going up through Central and North America, and connecting to the Eurasian transport systems via a tunnel under the Bering Strait.

such a huge task. Especially for the training of the youth, one can go back to the experience of Franklin Roosevelt's Civilian Conservation Corps—the CCC program—which contributed significantly to leading the United States out of the Depression in the '30s. Roosevelt called the CCC "the greatest peacetime movement this country has ever seen." It was created to address the dire lack of education and skills of the youth, a condition which in today's America takes the form of a very high level of drug addiction and drug-related crimes.

if the two complementary economies of the United States and China were to link up in this way.

Such United States-China cooperation would naturally not be limited to bilateral exchanges, but given the vast requirements for infrastructure, agriculture, and industrial development in the world, joint ventures almost anywhere in the world would provide a "win-win" perspective for the United States, China, and the third party country. Given the huge potential of the Belt and Road Initiative to develop into the World Land-Bridge proposed by the Schiller Institute in 2014, in the not so distant future a high-speed rail system could be built from the southern tip of South America in Chile and Argentina, all the way up through Central and North America, and connect to the Eurasian transport systems via a tunnel under the Bering Strait. This would provide the gateway for the United States to join the newly emerging Pacific-centered world. This would require vastly improving and expanding the Alaskan railroad corridors through Canada, and connecting that with a new rail system in the United States.

The Roosevelt Precedent

Such a perspective of approximately 40,000 miles of modern electrified rail, about half of which should be high-speed rail systems, would also mean an enormous investment in industrial production to supply the necessary goods and materials, as well as the training and education of the skilled labor, needed to accomplish

At the summit between President Trump and President Xi Jinping, they decided to set up four permanent dialogues, one of them devoted to economic issues. This group of experts could start to explore the project of the United States joining the BRI immediately.

The most important aspect of the concept of the United States joining with the Belt and Road Initiative, however, would be to inspire the whole population with hope for the future, a better future for generations to come—something which has been lost in the last five decades.

It would also demonstrate that President Trump's promise to "make America great again," does not contradict the interests of other countries, but that such win-win cooperation would move the entire world into a new era of human civilization. If the two largest economies of the world work together in this way, there will not be any problem on the planet which can not be solved.

If one studies the economic theory behind the tremendous success of the Chinese economic miracle of the last 30 years, one will find out that current Chinese economic policies, basing themselves on the education of its citizens, are very much in coherence with the Confucian principle of lifelong learning and innovation, and are actually very close to the economic principles of the American System of economy, as it was developed and implemented by Alexander Hamilton, John Quincy Adams, Henry Clay, Henry C. Carey, and Abraham Lincoln. All of these men understood that the

CasonVids/youtube

President Donald Trump hosts China President Xi Jinping at his Mar-a-Lago estate on April 6.

most important source of wealth of a country is the development of the creative powers of its own population. And therefore, they designed a system of economy that furthered exactly that, in order to catalyze the greatest rate of scientific and technological progress and innovation.

It is also fascinating that the real spiritual father of the American Republic, Benjamin Franklin, was to-tally excited and inspired by the writings of Confucius, from whom he took the conviction that the moral ennoblement of the individual was the absolute key for the improvement of society. Franklin based his own system of moral teaching on Confucius, which was decisive for the spirit of the founding of America. A very similar intellectual closeness existed between President Lincoln and the founding father of China.

The collaboration with the New Silk Road should therefore also have a cultural dimension, and exactly like the ancient Silk Road, should lead to an exchange of art and philosophy. It should do so to bring forward the best traditions and highest expression of humanity of each participating country, and in doing so, people will discover the unexpected beauty of the other cultures, and this knowledge will lead to admiration and will open new horizons. The epoch of a community of a shared future is within reach. If President Trump and President Xi Jinping join hands for this collaboration, both of them will have a place in history for having led Mankind to its true destiny.

Belt and Road Must Foster a Dialogue of Cultures, Zepp-LaRouche Tells China Audiences

by William Jones

May 24—Following her participation in the May 14-15 Belt and Road Forum in Beijing—called by President Xi Jinping to gather world leaders and the leaders of major think-tanks worldwide to discuss the Belt and Road Initiative (BRI), and to consolidate its achievements after its inception four years ago—Helga Zepp-LaRouche, the president of the German Schiller Institute, traveled to Nanjing, China.

There she gave a personal report-back from the Belt and Road Forum to the Phoenix Publishing Group, China's largest publishing house and the publishers of the Chinese version of the *EIR* Special Report, *The New Silk Road Becomes the World Land-Bridge*. "The Belt and Road has injected optimism into many countries," Zepp-LaRouche told the audience of about 200 at Phoenix headquarters, "and the momentum is unstoppable. But bringing it to full fruition will not be easy," she warned.

"Immediately after the Forum, the attacks against the Belt and Road escalated, combined with attacks against President Trump, who had sent a high-level delegation to the BRI Forum. The attacks were based on the absurd charges of collusion with Russia in the election," Zepp-LaRouche said. "After the Cold War, the British and their American allies wanted to create a unipolar world. And in doing so they have destroyed the Middle East and left it in a shambles." And this has precipitated the refugee crisis, the general reaction against "globalization," and the rise of right-wing movements. "The Belt and Road will bring about the creation of the World Land-Bridge which will connect all continents," she stressed. "And this is something we in the LaRouche organization have been fighting to achieve for over 40 years."

She described her fight and the fight of her husband, Lyndon LaRouche, over the past decades, to build a new world economic order. She described Mr. LaRouche's call for an International Development Bank in 1974, the Schiller Institute's fight for an African development plan in the late 1970s and 1980s, and the collaboration between LaRouche and Mexican President José López Portillo in the 1980s to rally the Latin

Helga Zepp-LaRouche, participating on May 15 in the Think Tank Summit associated with the Belt and Road Forum in Beijing.

Left: Guyana's Foreign Minister, Fred Wills, at the U.N. General Assembly.

Below left: Mexican President José López Portillo and Helga Zepp-LaRouche.

Below right: Indian Prime Minister Indira Gandhi.

Belt and Road Initiative," Zepp-LaRouche warned. She also underlined the tremendous opportunity that has arisen with the election of President Trump, who has expressed a willingness to move in the direction of Glass-Steagall and to rebuild the U.S.'s crumbling infrastructure. "This will create opportunities for China to make a contribution to the President's program," she said, but she warned that it cannot be accomplished simply by "market forces," but will require government involvement through the creation of a Hamiltonian bank or a similar infrastructure bank.

Zepp-LaRouche underlined how crucial it is

American nations around a just new world economic order.

Mrs. LaRouche also pointed to the hundreds of seminars held since the 1990s by the Schiller Institute calling for the creation of a New Silk Road. "Transforming the Belt and Road to a World Land-Bridge will realize politically for the first time a real future for all the people living on this planet, and will establish a new form of governance for the world," she said. "But to fully realize this, you must also study the ideas of my husband on the question of economics."

Zepp-LaRouche described the precarious state of the present international financial system, warning of the onset of a new financial crisis soon, unless measures are taken to revamp the present financial architecture, beginning with the implementation of the Glass-Steagall legislation which President Trump has repeatedly said that he intends to accomplish. "The financial crisis represents a grave threat to the

for the Belt and Road to become the launch-pad for that necessary dialogue of cultures that had also characterized the ancient Silk Road. "Each of the cultures along the Belt and Road must bring out its finest

National Archives

President Ronald Reagan announces his anti-missile Strategic Defense Initiative, on March 23, 1983.

achievements, in order to use these to create a cultural dialogue between the nations on the Belt and Road." She discussed the importance of Friedrich Schiller for German and Western culture, and compared this with the importance of Confucius for Chinese culture, showing the close similarities between the ideas of these two great thinkers, although separated in time by almost 2,000 years.

LaRouche's Decades of Struggle

Zepp-LaRouche was followed by Bill Jones, the Washington Bureau Chief of *EIR,* who showed Power-Point slides describing the various stages of the struggle of the LaRouche organization, starting from the destruction of the Bretton Woods system by President Nixon in 1971 and the 1970s launch of the Zero-Growth and Zero Population Growth by the genocidalist Club of Rome.

There was a fight against these developments at the Colombo conference of the Non-Aligned Movement and at the UN General Assembly, led by Guyana's Foreign Minister Fred Wills, who led the call for La-Rouche's International Development Bank. This proposal was finally realized with the recent establishment of the AIIB and the BRICS New Development Bank.

Jones also recalled the attempt by Lyndon LaRouche to bring President Reagan, who had adopted La-Rouche's concept of the Strategic Defense Initiative, into collaboration with Third World leaders like Indira Gandhi and José López Portillo in order to bring about a New World Economic Order. LaRouche's influence in the Reagan Administration led to a violent reaction by the neo-conservative circles around Vice President George H.W. Bush, who targeted LaRouche in a government-sponsored witch-hunt, which led to La-

Friedrich Schiller in discussion with friends.

Rouche's lengthy incarceration along with seven of his close associates.

Jones was followed at the podium by Professor Bao Shixiu, a professor of military science, who outlined for the audience the strategic importance of the Belt and Road, showing how it will allow China to overcome the traditional difficulties it has had with some countries like India and Japan.

Professor Bao underlined the seminal role of the LaRouches in bringing the Belt and Road initiative to the forefront of the world's attention, and the ongoing struggle of Lyndon and Helga LaRouche to overcome the opposition to it from the London-New York financial elites. Professor Bao also discussed both the economic and the strategic implications of the Belt and Road for China, which would help ensure a harmonious climate in the region and in the world, and allow China and all other countries to continue along their development paths.

The audience showed a great deal of interest, particularly in Zepp-LaRouche's call for the dialogue of cultures, and there was a heightened degree of interest in the work of Friedrich Schiller among the Phoenix staff, some of whom had a rather extensive exposure to the works of German classical culture.

Proceeding from Nanjing on the final leg of her trip, Zepp-LaRouche traveled to Shanghai for a series of meetings with several important Chinese think-tanks to discuss the issues raised in Nanjing. In Shanghai she was also interviewed by the *Shanghai Daily* and by the *China Daily.* Her consistent emphasis on creating a vibrant dialogue of cultures on the basis of the Belt and Road Initiative, struck a responsive chord among all her interlocutors, and elicited a commitment to exert even greater efforts in promoting such a dialogue.

II. Lyndon LaRouche on Manhattan

Lyndon LaRouche Calls for Committee On Manhattan Infrastructure

by Diane W. Sare

May 29—Last week, in response to a report from Manhattan Project organizers, Lyndon LaRouche proposed that a committee be created to do something about the alarming collapse of the Manhattan area transportation grid, and to "kick whoever needs it, to get it done."

As anyone who has attempted to travel into or through New York City will tell you, the roads in some areas, especially on toll plazas at the bridges, look like they were hit by a carpet bombing campaign. One couple returning from Staten Island to New Jersey destroyed three tires in one large pothole! And this, where each driver pays $15 just to cross the Hudson River! Driving is a high anxiety activity, which has become like an obstacle course in a war zone.

Then there's the subway. Aside from the fact that both the East River and Hudson River tunnels were built 107 years ago, in 1910, they were also damaged by Superstorm Sandy in 2013, which flooded them with salt water, which is corrosive, but also leaves a nasty, rock-hard residue around cables and wires, making "minor" repairs impossible. Some of the tunnels have been repaired, but the Canarsie Tunnel, built in 1924, which connects Manhattan to Brooklyn for 225,000 commuters each day, will have to be shut down for 15 months, beginning in 2019. The two tunnels crossing to New Jersey need to be replaced, and there is no other tunnel to absorb the traffic while new tunnels are being built.

Pennsylvania ("Penn") Station in Manhattan is already serving an average of 650,000 commuters per day, well over double the number of passengers for which it was built. Because it is so overloaded, and there are now so many delays—due to ancient switches and storm damage, among other problems—no one knows which track a train will be pulling into, until just a few minutes before it arrives. As a result, there is a mad swarm of rushing New Yorkers suddenly all trying to move to the same location at the same time. In early April, when a train derailed due to old tracks, 8 of the 21 tracks had to be shut down. The system is so run down, and so overloaded, that not only is there no redundancy, but any accident is likely to have a chain-reaction, multiplier effect.

Amtrak

Disruptions during repairs to LIRR and NJ Transit systems'aging track and infrastructure promise, in the words of Gov. Andrew Cuomo, a "Summer of Hell."

New York City is the center of the United States, the financial center, economic center, political center. A breakdown of transportation in the New York metropolitan area would be devastating for the nation. Here, Manhattan seen from the Port of Elizabeth, New Jersey.

A National Catastrophe

Repairs on Penn Station can no longer safely be delayed, so that, although there does not seem to be any comprehensive plan yet in place, as of July 7, 2017, up to 20% of the Long Island Railroad trains will no longer be going to Long Island, and there will be similar reductions in New Jersey Transit trains. This is being called, by New York State Governor Andrew Cuomo and others, the beginning of the "Summer of Hell." Supposedly the repairs are going to take "only" two months, but no one knows for sure. Moreover, although the partial shutdown begins on July 7, no plan has been announced to address the plight of commuters who need to get in and out of Manhattan each day. There are vague promises of ferries and buses, and proposals that some people should just start their work day at 4:00 am—but nothing concrete at all.

One of the tasks of LaRouche's proposed committee, should be to indicate the potential consequences of doing nothing about this nightmare, which clearly could implode into a catastrophe, including with great loss of life. When asked this question, rail transport corridor expert Hal Cooper said,

New York City is the center of the United States. It's the financial center; it's the economic center; it's the social center; it's the political center. If we don't repair the infrastructure, the ability of the people who work in New York—and I understand that's something like 1.8 million people who work in New York City [1.6 million commute into Manhattan each day to work, bringing the daytime population of Manhattan to over 3 million—ed.], and a large portion of them come from outside, either Westchester County or Rockland County, or from New Jersey or Long Island,— many of them wouldn't be able to get to work. An economic breakdown and collapse is going to happen, because so much of what is important in this country centers in New York City. And that is *absolutely essential*, and we will see a great breakdown if something is not done to correct the problem soon.

Integrate Manhattan into Belt & Road

In other words, the consequences of a breakdown of transportation in the New York metropolitan area would not only be catastrophic for the people in New

York, but would be devastating for the nation as a whole. This implosion must be prevented, but to do so requires urgent action, and even with urgent action, we will be unable to prevent certain damage from occurring.

A comprehensive plan to integrate Manhattan into China's Belt and Road Initiative is needed. That President Trump sent a high-level delegation to the Beijing conference in May, and has himself established a personal relationship with Chinese President Xi Jinping, is a promising beginning. Schiller Institute President Helga Zepp-LaRouche, who spoke on a think-tank panel at that Beijing conference, expressed the potential represented by Trump's commitment to spend $1 trillion on infrastructure, and to return to the American System of economics. She pointed out that Chinese estimates are that the United States needs something closer to $8 trillion in infrastructure investment, and the American Society of Civil Engineers has called for about $4.5 trillion—so Trump's proposal would definitely be a step in the right direction.

But there are obstacles to implementing the urgently needed projects. First, the U.S. Congress is stalling on reinstating the FDR-era Glass-Steagall Act, for which bills have been introduced in both the House and Senate, and for which the President has stated his support. But no one has thus far been willing to force it through. And second, the small-mindedness of the American people themselves who, after sixteen years of Bush and Obama, on top of the post-JFK rock-drug-sex counterculture— which is now *the* culture—barely consider the future at all, except as something they would like to avoid. Many of them are just drugging themselves into oblivion, when they should be grabbing their pitchforks and chasing down their Representatives with appropriate urgent demands.

There is also another important factor delaying such action, and that is the political witch-hunt against President Trump, directed from London. The hysteria being spouted in the U.S. news media about President Trump and his adminstration's relationship with anyone from Russia, and former President Barack Obama's and Hillary Clinton's campaigns to harass and scandalize the new administration, are highly destructive, not so much of Trump personally, who has demonstrated a fortunate willingness to fight, but of the opportunity that now greets the American people in the wake of the Beijing Belt and Road Forum.

Questions for the Committee

The committee that Mr. LaRouche has called for, will have to step back and look at Manhattan as if from outer space. With the impending doom of local breakdown, it can be challenging to consider where the United States and the world will be even 50 years from now, much less 100 or 1,000 years from now, but this is the kind of thinking that is required.

One factor, hopefully in the not-so-distant future, is the development of thermonuclear fusion power, which China is pursuing aggressively. With cheap, abundant, clean energy, what kind of transportation, manufacturing, water-management, and even food production becomes possible?

The Belt and Road is all about connectivity. Now that the Bayonne Bridge is going to be elevated, large freight container vessels will be able to get into the New Jersey ports of Elizabeth and Newark. What are the implications for trade? Not much if our rail system is in a shambles.

Should we have a rail transportation grid that connects our ports to our major cities? What about rail from Newark to China and Russia across the Bering Strait? What role would Detroit play in this? Could New York City become a manufacturing center again? How will we connect the Port of Elizabeth to the high-tech areas of Connecticut and Long Island? What about building the storm surge barrier that should have been erected before Sandy? Shouldn't those industries in Long Island, New Jersey, and Connecticut that contributed so much to the Apollo Project, be revived, to become part of NASA's collaboration with China on a mission to Mars, and in establishing an industrial base on the Moon?

New York City and the contiguous areas have a high density of capable people and also of potentially capable people, if there were a crash program to train them. These are the questions that the people of the United States need to urgently consider, not whether Jared Kushner had a meeting with the Russian Ambassador (which would probably have been a good idea).

LaRouche's Four Laws provide the parameters for the needed crash program. Now we must assemble a committee of experts who can fill in the details, and by so doing, transform the way that New Yorkers think about the current catastrophe. Remember, in Chinese, the character for crisis is also the character for opportunity.

NEW YORK TRANSIT CRISIS

Don't 'Repair' the System; Join the Belt and Road Initiative

by Robert Ingraham

May 29—In a series of writings and actions between 1789 and 1793, Alexander Hamilton defined and promulgated a new, revolutionary Principle of National Public Credit. His urgent concern was to secure the survival of the new nation. He was successful. But Hamilton was also driven by a higher purpose, a future-oriented vision. Hamilton created an economic approach which subsumed, within its species dynamic, the questions of Labor, Productivity & Creativity. This, in Hamilton's view, would become the bedrock for the new Republic.

It is precisely this issue of human productive and creative potential which has defined much of Lyndon LaRouche's life work and which is set forth most succinctly in his 2014 economic action plan, *The Four New Laws to Save the U.S.A. Now!* The principles, as developed by LaRouche in the *Four New Laws,* are fully coherent with the vision set forth by Alexander Hamilton at the time of the nation's founding.

Today, we are presented with an historic opportunity, one which holds out the promise for a global realization of the vision which Hamilton represented in his own time. The proceedings of the May 14-15 Belt and Road Forum in Beijing have now placed on the table—for all of humanity—a perspective for world-wide peace and economic development: not incremental development held hostage by the monetary *diktats* of London and Wall Street, but boundless leaps in the development of the human condition. The staggering progress that has been made by China within less than a decade almost blinds the eye as a beacon demonstrating what is now possible on a global scale.

wikipedia

The Long Island Rail Road concourse at Penn Station.

The subject of this article is the transportation crisis which is now affecting the New York Metropolitan Area, particularly as that relates to rail transport. What must be kept in mind throughout the reading of this article are the global developments, and the enormous potential for economic development, within which this New York crisis must be viewed. The New York rail system is at a point of breakdown, and is increasingly dysfunctional and dangerous. Yet, only a fool would propose as a goal to "make the trains run on time," and even many of the necessary improvements which have been proposed remain too timid and limited compared to what is actually needed. A bolder vision is required, and is now possible.

In this article we will look first at some aspects of the crisis in New York. This will be followed by a brief overview of some of what has been accomplished in China, concluding with some remarks as to what should be the actual approach to both New York's and the nation's transportation needs.

I. The New York Mess

New York City's Penn Station is the busiest rail terminal in the world.[1] It handles 650,000 commuters per day, which is greater than the entire population of Baltimore or Milwaukee and is more than double the combined daily traffic through JFK, LaGuardia, and Newark airports. It is also triple the capacity the station was designed for. Currently, it is teetering on the brink of total breakdown. In his January 2016 State of the State speech, New York Governor Andrew Cuomo described Penn Station: "Penn Station is decrepit and it's an affront to riders to use it. It is dirty; it is dingy; it is dark; it's terrible." Cuomo's remarks are an understatement. Penn Station and the trains and system it services are dangerous, operate under conditions that are increasingly inhuman, and function day-to-day under near-crisis conditions.

Not only is Penn Station during rush hour a terrifying, other-worldly experience in which the human herd becomes indistinguishable from cattle in the stockyards, but the real rot is hidden below the surface, underground in the tunnels and along the tracks. Much of the infrastructure—the tracks, the roadbeds, the ties, the signals, the drainage systems—are seventy-five or one hundred years old, or in the case of the tunnels and bridges, even older.

Earlier this year, on March 24 and April 3, there were two derailments in Penn Station, one of which caused a crash between two trains. The most revealing thing about these derailments is that they both took place at very low speeds. This was not a case of trains traveling too fast for conditions. It was simply that the underlying track, ties and ballast were worn out and could no longer support the trains. These two derailments combined, resulted in delays and cancellations up and down the corridor between Boston and Washington, D.C., disrupting the entire transit system of the

Xinhua/David Torres

Rescue personnel are busy working above-ground near the site of derailment, May 2, 2014. A train carrying some 1,000 passengers and heading towards Manhattan ran off the tracks, resulting in 19 injuries.

Northeast. In addition, almost half of the local rail lines to Long Island and New Jersey were knocked out of commission for four consecutive days, resulting in transit chaos throughout the region.

Even earlier this year, on Jan. 4, more than 100 people were hurt when a Long Island Rail Road train struck a bumper at Atlantic Terminal in Brooklyn.

These incidents are portents of a disaster that is certain to come unless something is done. In 1940 the total population of the greater New York Metropolitan Region was ten million. By 1960 it was over sixteen million, and today, the figure is twenty-three million, and that figure is expected to rise to thirty million within the next twenty to thirty years. Yet, the combined rail and subway system which services the region is not much different than what existed in 1940. Track mileage, the number of stations, the number of trains are nearly the same. The only thing that has increased— dramatically—is the number of passengers. If anything, despite some improvements here and there, decades of decay, cost-cutting, and austerity measures have rotted out the rail system from the inside.

Massive population and economic growth has taken place in Hudson, Essex, and Bergen counties, Westchester, Rockland, Nassau, and Suffolk. Yet the transit system to service it travels over infrastructure that is both woefully inadequate and old and dangerous. Historically, much of the damage that was done to the com-

---

1. Penn Station is the terminus for both the Long Island Rail Road (the busiest commuter railroad in the world) and New Jersey Transit (the second busiest commuter railroad in the world). It also services all Amtrak trains traveling between Boston and Washington, D.C.

muter lines servicing New York City occurred following the 1970 bankruptcy of the Penn Central Railroad, which resulted in a decades-long process of cost-cutting, asset-stripping, and a failure to maintain even basic infrastructure. This policy of enforced decay has never been fully reversed.

The New York City Subway

The New York City Subway currently handles 1.8 *billion* passengers per year. For the entirety of the 20th Century, it serviced the largest volume of passengers of any urban subway system in the world, until it was recently surpassed by both Shanghai and Beijing. Daily ridership is near six million passengers (larger than the populations of Houston and Chicago combined).

wikipedia

Flooded subways after Hurricane Sandy: MTA Bridges and Tunnels workers pumping 43 million gallons of water out of each of the tubes of the Brooklyn-Battery Tunnel.

The current state of the New York subway system is far worse than the commuter railroads. The subway system is 110 years old. It is decaying. A significant portion of the infrastructure is more than seventy-five years old. Since 2000 there have been six major train derailments and many minor ones. Following a deadly crash between two trains on the Williamsburg Bridge in 1995, speeds were reduced on all of the subway lines, and today the entire subway system operates at an average speed of 17 mph (27 km/h). Rails break, trains break, and tracks and stations get flooded out during heavy rains. Power outages and other electrical problems now regularly cause shutdowns of entire lines. Parts of the system are even closed during snow storms, something which never occurred during its first seventy-five years of operation. Stations are awash with garbage and rats. Massive delays, which disrupt the commutes of hundreds of thousands, are increasing.

One of the worst problems within the system is the signal system, much of which was built before World War II. The signal system directs traffic for the entire schedule of thousands of trains. Most of New York's subway system still relies on antiquated technology, known as "block signaling," to coordinate the movement of trains. Signaling problems are one of the major causes for train delays within the New York system.

Most modern subway systems outside of the United States have switched to using a computerized signal system known as Communications-Based Train Control, or CBTC. CBTC is a railway signaling system that makes use of the telecommunications between the train and track equipment for traffic management and infrastructure control. CBTC is far more precise, makes it possible to reduce the amount of space between trains, and is safer because trains can be stopped automatically.

New York's quest to install the new system began in 1991, after a subway derailment at Union Square in Manhattan killed five people. Now, twenty-six years later, only one line (the Canarsie L line) has installed the modern signals. A second line, the No. 7, is slated to begin operating with the new signals by the end of this year. At this rate it will take more than fifty years to upgrade the entire system. It is estimated that the entire upgrade could cost more than $20 billion. Complicating the problem is the fact that none of the subway cars built before 2000 are CBTC compatible, so a great deal of new rolling stock will have to be purchased.

In October 2012, Hurricane Sandy delivered a near death blow to the subway system. Many subway tunnels were inundated with floodwater (seawater). The subway closed completely for two days and then reopened with limited service, but a great deal of the infrastructure was seriously damaged and much of it has still not been repaired. The storm flooded nine of the system's fourteen underwater tunnels, many subway lines, and several subway yards, and completely destroyed a portion of the IND Rockaway Line and much of the South Ferry terminal station. Whole sections of the system were closed for months, and several stations and lines have yet to reopen.

Despite the obvious and precarious condition of the subway system, that same system is now being forced, like Penn Station, to deal with a massive surge in ridership. Whole sections of the system, particularly in Manhattan, are operating every day way beyond capacity, carrying far more passengers than the system was designed for even under optimum conditions. In addition to the daily flood of commuters who use the subway once they are in the city, New York City's own population is growing, rising 4.4 percent from 8.18 million in 2010 to 8.54 million in 2016, with expectations that a future population of 9 million is a certainty. Facing this reality, no limited approach to "repair" the subways will prevent the entire system from grinding to a halt.

II. China's 'Decade of Miracles'

Less than a decade ago, China had yet to connect any of its cities by bullet train. As of today, China has completed the construction of 22,000 km (14,000 miles) of high-speed rail (HSR), a length that is more than the rest of the world's high-speed rail tracks combined. HSR now extends to twenty-nine of the coun-

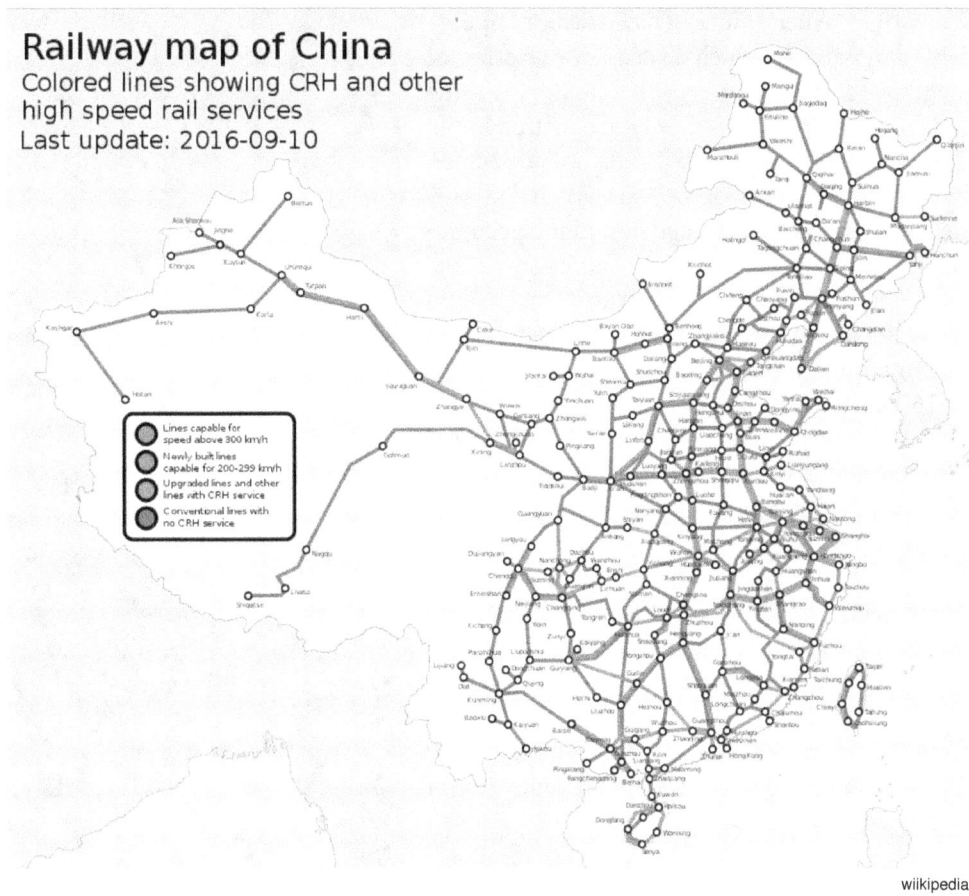

Railway map of China
Colored lines showing CRH and other high speed rail services
Last update: 2016-09-10

Lines capable for speed above 300 km/h
Newly built lines capable for 200-299 km/h
Upgraded lines and other lines with CRH service
Conventional lines with no CRH service

wiikipedia

try's thirty-three provinces and carries more than 1.44 billion passengers per year. But this is just the beginning. China is planning to build another 16,000 km by 2025. China has a four-by-four grid at present: four big north-south and east-west lines. Its new plan is to construct an eight-by-eight grid by 2035, encompassing an eventual network of 45,000 km of high-speed track.

China is building a "high-speed rail economy." A major focus is to extend the lines westward into the interior, to develop many new cities and economic centers. As a result of this effort, in the more thinly populated regions of Xinjiang, Gansu, Qinghai, Sichuan, Yunnan, Guangxi, Inner Mongolia, and Heilongjiang, there has already been astonishing urban growth alongside the tracks. At regular intervals—almost wherever there are stations, even if seemingly in the middle of nowhere—thickets of newly built offices, factories and residential blocks are rising from the ground. All of this has been accompanied by the development of energy grids and water, communication, and other infrastructure.

China's efforts to improve rail service actually date

from 1997, when it initiated a series of "Speed-Up" campaigns, which lasted—in a series of stages—for ten years, as preparatory to the launching of true high-speed rail construction in 2007. In 1997 Chinese railroads operated at an average speed of 48 km/h (30 mph), and no two major cities were connected by a high-speed rail line. Beginning with the construction of the Guangzhou-Shenzhen Railway, and then moving through a series of other projects, China began to upgrade the speed of its railways, first to 160 km/h and then to 200 km/h. Today, China defines high-speed rail as trains that operate at a minimum of 250 km/h, and the average speed on its system is 300 km/h.

Initially, China's early high-speed trains were imported or built under technology transfer agreements with foreign train-makers including Alstom, Siemens, Bombardier, and Kawasaki. As of today, Chinese engineers have re-designed train components and the newer indigenous trains are manufactured in China by the CRRC Corporation—the world's largest supplier of rail transit equipment.

A stunning accomplishment was the completion of the Beijing-Shanghai High-Speed Railway (Jinghu High-Speed Railway), a 1,318 km (819 mi) high-speed railway that connects China's two largest cities. Construction began on April 18, 2008, and the line opened on June 30, 2011. The whole project took just over three years. This is the longest high-speed line ever constructed in a single phase. Although capable of going faster, the non-stop train from Beijing South to Shanghai Hongqiao currently operates at an average speed of 300 km/h, and the trip takes four hours and forty-eight minutes. Additionally, a slower class of trains running at 250 km/h (155 mph) operates along the line, making more (local) stops and charging lower fares. By comparison, in 1990 the fastest rail link between Beijing and Shanghai took more than seventeen hours.

Almost all rail operations are handled by the China Railway Corporation (CR), a state-owned company created in March 2013. China's high-speed lines are operated by China Railway High-Speed (CRH), a subsidiary of CR. In addition to the high-speed Passenger Dedicated Lines (PDLs), one of China Railways' primary concerns has been to increase freight hauling.

Xinhua/Liu Yongzhen

The first commercial bullet train set off from Beijing South Railway Station on the Beijing-Shanghai High-Speed Railway, June 30, 2011.

Much of this effort has already been integrated with the HSR lines, resulting, for example, in an increase in freight capacity by fifty million tons per year on the Beijing-Shanghai line.

Much of these developments have been accompanied by significant technological and engineering improvements throughout the system, including double-tracking, electrification, and the introduction of ballastless tracks, which allow for smoother train rides at high speeds and can withstand heavy use without warping.

Subways

China is a nation of almost 1.4 billion people, and it has fourteen cities with a population of more than five million. Simultaneously with its development of HSR during the last decade, China has also acted aggressively to deal with the challenge of urban gridlock.

Before 1990, just three of the country's cities had subway lines: Beijing, Hong Kong, and Tianjin. By 2020, that number is expected to grow to more than forty cities. Shanghai and Beijing have seen tremendous growth, their subway lines now serving 2 billion and 1.84 billion riders respectively a year, the two busiest in the world.

In the past four years alone, Beijing's subway added three brand new lines and significantly expanded five existing ones, opening more than 100 stations since 2012. Currently, the Beijing subway has 19 lines, 345 stations and 574 km (357 mi) of track in operation, and they are currently constructing six new fully automated lines which will add another 300 km (190 mi). All of this is being done with the most advanced technology, including the use of domestically developed communications-based train control systems (CBTC), discussed above. In Beijing, China is in the process of creating the longest fully automated subway network in the world.

In addition to the escalating construction of thousands of kilometers of subway rail lines, China has also embarked on the development of low- and medium-speed maglev trains for urban and suburban use. The first of these lines in Changsha, Hunan province, has now been operating for a year, and a second line in Beijing will begin operation this year.

These two lines are just the beginning. In Hunan province, the manufacturing company CRRC Tangshan Co, Ltd. has begun mass production of these systems. Other companies, in Hebei province and elsewhere, are also involved in this production. These trains, along with the infrastructure which supports them, are all domestically designed and manufactured. Negotiations are now ongoing to expand the use of these "medium-low speed" maglevs to many other cities throughout China.

The Changsha maglev is able to reach speeds of 120

Xinhua/Long Hongtao
China's first domestically produced middle-to-low-speed magnetically levitated (maglev) rail line in Changsha shuttles between Changsha's south railway station and the airport.

km/h, but its average operational speed is 100 km/h. Some might consider this slow, but when one compares this to the average speed of a New York City subway train (27 km/h), it is quite respectable. According to a recent statement by a representative of CRRC Tangshan Co, it will deliver the first of a next generation of medium speed maglev trains later this year with a top speed of 160 km/h, a development which can only accelerate the deployment of these systems.

These medium-low speed maglev systems cost less than twenty-five percent of the cost to build traditional subways, and they are even less expensive than the much slower and inefficient "light-rail" systems. In addition, they are quieter, take up less space, and are safer.

The Return of Maglev

Since the opening of the Shanghai Maglev in 2004, maglev has failed to penetrate China's high-speed rail development despite an unmatched advantage in speed, and since 2007 all of the high-speed rail projects have utilized traditional wheel-to-rail technology. One of the reasons for this has been the high cost of construction and maintenance for the ultra-high-speed (430 km/h) maglev systems, but an even bigger obstacle stems from the refusal by Siemens and ThyssenKrupp, the German manufacturers of the Shanghai line, to share technology with their Chinese clients or to source production into China. This was something that the Chinese refused to accept, and was likely the primary consideration in their decision to not move forward with maglev after 2004.

This situation has now changed. The successful work in the domestic (China-built) development of medium-low speed maglev trains has contributed greatly to China's mastery of the technology, and earlier this year the Chinese government announced that it will be spending 3 billion yuan in 2017 to develop high-speed maglev systems. China's CRRC Corp has also announced that it is beginning research and development on a 600 km/h maglev train and would build a 5 km test track, with a target date of 2020 for the development of an operational system. China's ultimate goal is to export this technology, including both medium-low speed and high-speed maglev systems. An official at the Hunan maglev project recently stated that observation teams have already visited such countries as Singapore, Germany, and Brazil.

III. New York Must Join the Belt and Road

There are several initiatives now underway, both official and unofficial, to address the transit crisis in New York. These include Amtrak's current Gateway Project, centering on the construction of a new tunnel for rail lines under the Hudson River, which would double the capacity of Penn Station; and the Jan. 13, 2016 announcement by New York Governor Andrew Cuomo of his $100 billion "Built to Lead" infrastructure initiative for the State of New York, which includes $3 billion to rebuild and rehabilitate the Penn Station complex. There are also significant private initiatives and proposals, including that put forward by ReThinkNYC which focuses on a proposal to transform Penn Station from a terminal to a "through station," linking up New Jersey Transit with the Long Island Rail Road as part of one "through" transit system. Unlike many other "transit planners," the ReThinkNYC proposal envisions a truly integrated regional transit system.

In his recent presentation to the LaRouche PAC Manhattan Meeting on May 27, international rail expert Hal Cooper stated the necessary approach this way:

The subway system is in an increasingly fragile state. The signaling and communications systems are going to have to be repaired; the tunnel problems that were talked about on the Number 7 line are certainly very, very real and have to be addressed. I understand that the East Side access project, building from Sunnyside Yard over in Queens to 63rd Street and Park Avenue in Manhattan is moving ahead. It's been started, and that is a critical element.

We are going to have to build train loops in New Jersey, and we're going to have to build a new tunnel under the Hudson River. We have a similar problem over at the tunnels on the East Side, but not as serious. And we have an electrification problem in that we have non-compatible systems for the Long Island Rail Road, Metro North, and Amtrak and New Jersey Transit, that we're going to have to fix at some point.[2]

We have to make Penn Station a completely through station and we're going to need to be able to go from Grand Central to Penn Station and in reverse, and also be able to have a loop. And we need to expand the Long Island Rail Road connections. One of those possibilities is taking the present PATH from the World Trade Center, extending under Lower Manhattan, extending it under the southern end of the East River so that it ultimately connects with the Brooklyn Borough Hall and Jamaica Station in Queens, which then gives people direct access to the airport and also takes some of the pressure off the trains coming into Penn Station. And we're going to have to align railroads whether we want to or not, and that's a very important factor.

We've got to fix the subway system; we've got to fix the Amtrak; we've got to have new bases for turning trains around and maintaining them; we have to make Penn Station completely a through station, and that means we've got to build a lot of new infrastructure. At Penn Station we've got to get the Farley Post Office converted into the Amtrak facility, and the present Penn

_____

2. Trains in the New York metropolitan region run on five different types of power. What this means in practical terms is that the train cars used by Metro-North and Long Island Rail Road can't run in New Jersey, and vice-versa, making a unified system very difficult to integrate.

Xinhua

China is working with other nations to transform the world. Workers lay track during the celebration of the completion of 100 km of track for the Chinese-financed and -designed railway project linking Abuja and Kaduna, Nigeria, June 14, 2014.

Station for the commuter rail. It needs to happen, rather than talking about it needing to happen. And that's a very critical thing, that right now it isn't on the agenda for being discussed in the way that it should be. And all that needs to be taken care of.

Think Like the Chinese

Were he alive to witness today's events, Alexander Hamilton would immediately recognize the genius driving the recent transformation of China. China's development of its high-speed rail systems, its maglev systems, and its subway systems should not be viewed as a "transportation" policy. All of the advances that have been made, have taken place over a ten-year span during which the Chinese have lifted 700 million of their own people out of poverty; during a span where they have initiated the most ambitious space program of any nation since the demise of the U.S. manned space program; and during a span in which they have now joined with scores of other nations and billions of human beings in the Belt and Road Initiative for worldwide physical economic development.

China is not simply building transit. They are building the world and building up the people of the world. Hamilton would recognize this. Lyndon LaRouche and his wife Helga Zepp-LaRouche recognize this. The problem in America today is two fold. First, there is simply a lack of vision. A smallness. Even those, like Gov. Cuomo, who talk about "great projects," think too small. Most infrastructure proposals aim to fix immediate problems, or at best, to deal with projected demand twenty-five years into the future. Any competent approach to infrastructure must include a study of La-Rouche's concept of "economic platforms" and must plan for where we need to be at least one hundred years (a minimum of three generations) into the future. This includes transportation, energy, water, and all other forms of infrastructure, science and industry.

The second, even bigger, problem is that almost all of the people on the American side, who are involved in these types of discussions, are prisoners of the Wall Street monetarist system and mentality. They can't figure out how to finance great projects. They constantly ask, "Where is the money going to come from?" They don't understand Hamiltonian Public Credit. They don't understand how Roosevelt did what he did. They—and all of us—live within a system in which the interests of financial speculators come first. America needs a minimum of $10 trillion dollars to transform its infrastructure and to build a future. Under the current financial dictatorship of London and Wall Street, that will never happen.

The concerns raised in this article are not exclusive to New York City. This is not an article for "New Yorkers." All of the issues raised here are representative, in one way or another, of similar crises throughout the nation, and the lack of vision and the submissiveness to the usurious policies of Wall Street are a national phenomenon. Look to China! There they are transforming their nation, their people, their culture, and they are working with other nations to transform the world. We can and must be part of this.

Every Day Counts In Today's Showdown To Save Civilization

That's why you need EIR's **Daily Alert Service**, a strategic overview compiled with the input of Lyndon LaRouche, and delivered to your email 5 days a week.

The election of Donald Trump to the Presidency of the Untied States has launched a new global era whose character has yet to be determined. The Obama-Clinton drive toward confrontation with Russia has been disrupted--but what will come next?

Over the next weeks and months there will be a pitched battle to determine the course of the Trump Administration. Will it pursue policies of cooperation with Russia and China in the New Silk Road, as the President-Elect has given some signs of? Will it follow through against Wall Street with Glass-Steagall?

The opposition to these policies will be fierce. If there is to be a positive outcome to this battle, an informed citizenry must do its part--intervening, educating, inspiring. That's why you need the EIR Daily Alert more than ever.

TUESDAY, NOVEMBER 22, 2016

Volume 3, Number 65

EIR Daily Alert Service

P.O. Box 17390, Washington, DC 20041-0390

- Only Global Solutions, Based on New Principles, Can Work
- Tulsi Gabbard Meets with Donald Trump Regarding Syria
- Robert Kagan Throws in the Towel, Complains U.S. Is Becoming 'Solipsistic'
- War Party Moving To Preempt Trump-Putin Reset
- Syrian Army Makes More Progress in Aleppo
- Duterte Gives OK to Nuclear Power for Philippines
- Europe Will Suffer from Maintaining Russia Sanctions
- Former Chilean Diplomat Confirmed, 'We Will Joyfully Welcome Xi Jinping'
- Duterte and Putin Establish Philippines-Russia Cooperation
- François Fillon, Pro-Russian Thatcherite, Wins First Round of French Right-Wing Presidential Primary

EDITORIAL

Only Global Solutions, Based on New Principles, Can Work

III. LaRouche in 2010: Replace A Monetary by a Credit System

AUGUST 26, 2010

THE ECONOMIC PAST IS NOW BEHIND US!

Money or Credit?

by Lyndon H. LaRouche, Jr.

It has happened as I had forecast it would occur within this relatively narrow interval of time. It occurred during the closing business days of that past week, in a time short of four decades, that since August 1971, when matters have now come to today's narrow, panic-stricken close. The effect has been, essentially, world-wide.

This happened inside the U.S.A., because nothing which I had prescribed, as in 2007, since a time when nothing that should have been done by the U.S. government, had been done to prevent this terrible present crisis from happening. The present world monetary system had been poised, until now, to enter a certain kind of hyper-inflationary collapse—unless we acted now to prevent it, a collapse which would amount to an approximation of what had happened to Germany, by itself, back in 1923. At this present time, the threatened effect is not to one nation by itself, as in 1923 Germany; it is world-wide. It is, in fact, a threat which, if now permitted to continue much longer, would mean an accelerating rate of plunge into an early, world-wide collapse, a collapse comparable to, but worse than, the "New Dark Age" of Europe's Fourteenth Century.[1]

As I had warned in July 2007, that collapse had to be prevented beforehand; whatever the form of prevention which we must take now; no delay is excusable. No escape can occur until President Barack Obama had been safely, peacefully, and suddenly removed from office. Otherwise, if he remains in office much longer, the U.S.A. and much more will soon be doomed. Already, a week or so ago, the cabal around this President had already unleashed the surge into what is presently a hellish, global, hyperinflation, unless we introduce the radical change in policies needed to stop it. We must quench those fires of potential hyperinflation now, or it will soon be too late to prevent the new holocaust now descending upon our planet.

Therefore, for reasons such as those, not only in our United States, but throughout the world as a whole, the Anglo-American trans-Atlantic sector is now poised at the brink of the greatest magnitude of combined monetary and physical collapse in all modern history to pres-

---

1. As I shall emphasize this fact at an appropriately later point within the body of this report, most people are still unable to recognize the distinction between the practices of merely "predicting," and competent "forecasting." In brief, the fact of the matter is, that it is, usually only the superstitious people who "predict" a statistical date-certain for a crucial turn in events. Admittedly, in my first publicized forecast, a short-term forecast of a major recession to strike about February-March 1957, which I made in July 1956, special factors centered in the automobile industry at that time, allowed for such a precise dating. Otherwise, barring such extraordinary circumstances as that, competent economists,

who are, admittedly, rare these days, rely on forecasting what were the consequences of not only failing to foresee, but, failing to correct for the consequences embedded in choosing, or simply defining a specific area of physical-economic space-time within which a change of state of a social process, for either the better, or the worse, must be foreseen. For reasons which I have already presented, repeatedly, the personal, pathological traits of President Barack Obama would prevent him from abandoning those stubborn choices which would, themselves, ensure an early, chain-reaction collapse of the present world monetary-financial system. Notably, the presently "popular," but incompetent, customary methods of statistical forecasting, are predicated upon the presumptions of a Paolo Sarpian form of indifferentism, such as those of his follower Adam Smith, that in opposition to the existence of any actually efficient and knowable expressions of universal physical principles.

ent date.

Thus, at the beginning of the presently new week, a certain failed personality, U.S. President Barack Obama, was being relegated by the wise to his presently impending, early departure from the U.S. Presidency. The only sane option for a continuation of civilization on our planet, now, would be to abandon a presently, utterly failed, global, monetarist system, and to replace it by a credit system of the form which had been intended by the U.S. Presidency of Franklin Delano Roosevelt. This change, from that monetary system which is now destroying our nation, to enter a physical-economic recovery under a credit-system, demands some crucially significant kinds of urgently needed changes in the economic organization of not only the U.S. economy itself, but the planet considered in the large.

The prospect of the actual launching of what had been the 1964 NAWAPA project now sets the pace, with its included advances in certain technologies, for a sudden, mass, high-technology employment used as a means for rescuing the United States, among others, from the global catastrophe which a continuation of the mass-murderous, puppet-government of British imperial puppet and U.S. President Barack Obama would mean.

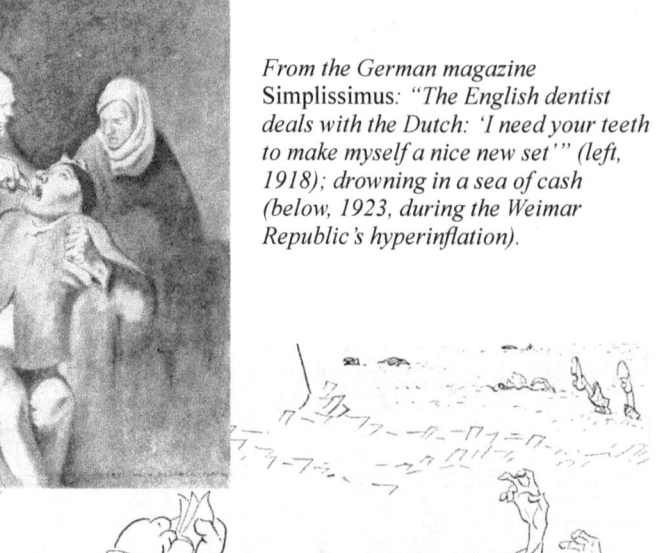

From the German magazine Simplissimus: "The English dentist deals with the Dutch: 'I need your teeth to make myself a nice new set'" (left, 1918); drowning in a sea of cash (below, 1923, during the Weimar Republic's hyperinflation).

The Task Now Before Us:

The crucial proposition is this:

Could our United States of America survive the successive efforts to destroy this republic, which Presidents George W. Bush, Jr. and Barack Obama have combined to do, thus far? The answer is: "Not if Barack Obama is still serving as President during a mere few months, or even some weeks just ahead."

Therefore, the fact is, that unless Obama is soon re-moved from the Presidency, it were likely, that not only were the U.S.A. soon finished as a nation; the economy of the entire trans-Atlantic region would also go down, quickly, and the doom of Asian nations were then virtually an ensuing certainty, as well. If my proposed, relatively immediate ouster of President Barack Obama were to be carried out as I have specified, the remaining question would then be: "How will the required recovery work?" In that case, the proper choice of leading subject for debate among the minds of the world's leading governments would be: "What is the essential, systemic difference, if any, between a 'money system' and a 'credit system'?"

If those conditions are met, the conclusion which should have been reached, very soon, among even the few of those governments which will have succeeded in selecting the proper answer, will be expressed as a choice in favor of a "credit system." This crucial decision will be of the form: "We must concede, that the choice must be the immediate replacement of a monetary system by a virtually global credit system."

That decision would be successful. No other would.

The adoption of such a reform in systems of, and among respectively sovereign nations, would depend, strictly, upon four measures taken in rapid succession:

1. President Obama must be "resigned." He had been a failed personality, in the sense that his quality of personal fault is essentially the same mental illness as that of the Emperor Nero and Adolf Hitler, a fault which led their respective nations to comparable disasters, and even much of the world. We must not delay, by waiting, like silly sidewalk spectators, for that inevitable end to be delivered.
2. The next step, as soon as President Obama is being retired from office, will be a summary installation of an exact copy of the 1933 U.S. Glass-Steagall Act as being an immediate and permanent measure of global reform.
3. An alliance of certain major and other sovereign, concurring nation-states, will be launched in the form of a global, fixed-exchange-rate credit system, copying, thus, what had been President Franklin Roosevelt's 1944 Bretton Woods intention for the post-war world.
4. A series of major programs of long-ranging, and far-reaching investments in infrastructure-building, representing, thus, a program typified by the immediate launching of a full NAWAPA development, both on Earth and as its reflection in the nearer regions of our Solar System. This will be a program conducted through cooperation among willing sovereign nations. This program will serve as the driver of an accelerating rate of increase of the productive powers of labor throughout the remaining decades of this presently still-young century.

As a study of the implications of an immediate initiation of a NAWAPA program now, shows, the actual launching of the NAWAPA mission, under those conditions, now, could stop, and even reverse the presently oncoming dive into what, unless stopped would be the deepest and longest of depressions in modern world history. In fact, such reforms as these would rescue the planet from that deep dive into a breakdown-crisis which was already set into motion a few weeks past, by the Obama Administration and its accomplices within the U.S. Federal Reserve System.

In that case, in respect to principles of law, the governing policy of urgently needed reform shall be, that "mere money has no intrinsic value anywhere on this planet! None!"

Strictly speaking, the kind of "value" which might be attributed to the "money" of leading nations, then, would be premised on the reality, that money carries nothing as much as a "political value" assigned by a society, rather than a physical-economic one. Thus, the uttering of credit by and among sovereign national partners, is to be done, politically, for their individual and mutual, immediate and long-term benefits.

For this arrangement to succeed, that arrangement must be made under a fixed-exchange-rate credit-system; which will then serve as the principal, physical-economic driver of an accelerating rate of increase of the physically productive powers of labor, not only within sovereign nations, but among a community of sovereigns.

The NAWAPA Example

This change must be effected in accord with the notion of "infrastructure" which is typified by my initiative for the immediate launching of the realization of a "full-throated" and up-to-date installation of the NAWAPA program.

We must come to think in terms of qualitative leaps in the productive organization of cultures and their societies. We must come to think in terms of the Promethean terms of qualitative advances identified with leaps in orders of "energy-flux density."

For example, the presently preliminary stages of man's progress toward man's prospective "colonization" of Mars, compel us to rise to the platform of thermonuclear fusion. That, in turn, requires a shift of thinking from a science of particle physics, from a science of particles, to a science of singularities in an interplanetary space which is never empty space, but always richly dense with cosmic radiation, including that by, and among living persons.

That is to emphasize, that the properly corrected use of the term "infrastructure," is in agreement with the notion of "infrastructure" which I have supplied in earlier publications on this subject. In these publications, I have emphasized that the corrected use of that term be applied to the range of successive, qualitative advances in the introduction of higher qualities of "platforms," as

U.S. Army Corps of Engineers/Bob Heims

The North American Water and Power Alliance (NAWAPA) is the foremost plan for global infrastructure development, now on the table for immediate adoption. The project would divert water that currently flows north into the Arctic, to the south, where it would make the biosphere bloom throughout western Canada and the United States and northern Mexico. Shown is the Dalles Dam in Oregon.

typified by the succession of: maritime cultures, riparian systems, national, continental, and intercontinental railway cultures, nuclear-fission culture and thermonuclear fusion cultures, and the still higher culture of the integration of nearby space of our Solar System according to the same general direction of qualitative leaps in "energy-flux density," in ordering the creation of the successively higher orders of the platforms by means of which achievement of the higher qualities of productivity is to be accomplished.

Such are the specific conclusions which must be reached by those nations which will have come to prefer the use of "money" as limited, specifically, to the notions associated with a credit-system of the type specific to the beginning of what had been that of a type specific to the roots of the later U.S. economy in what had been, originally, associated with the use of the "Pinetree shilling" introduced under the original charter of the Massachusetts Bay settlement. That was the economy which had succeeded marvelously until those suc-

cessive interventions by England's King James II and William of Orange which had crushed the settlement's rights to trappings of sovereignty in matters of economy.

Even after the U.S. had secured its independence by war, the ability of the British empire to apply crushing force to a U.S.A. left isolated by the political collapses of its former, war-time, European allies, led it to suffer repeatedly under rapacious British interventions into its internal and foreign affairs, and, often, even under Presidents who were agents of the British East India Company's footholds within the U.S. economy and political system. It was not until the U.S.A.'s victory over Lord Palmerston's British puppet known as the Confederacy, that the U.S.A. could sometimes challenge British imperial power effectively. That advantage was largely dissipated by a series of assassinations of Presidents through that killing of William McKinley which brought a series of British and Wall Street puppets, such as Theodore Roosevelt, Woodrow Wilson, Calvin

Coolidge, and Herbert Hoover, until the time that the U.S. and its Constitution regained its certain degree of independence under President Franklin D. Roosevelt; but, then, lost much of it under President Harry S Truman, and under the still radiating effects of that assassination of President John F. Kennedy which cleared the decks for London's steering the U.S.A. into the prolonged, ruinous war in Indo-China from which the U.S.A.'s sovereignty has never fully recovered, to the present day.

The essential misfortune on account of U.S. Presidents and other politically influential figures who were virtually British puppets, was, in part, a reflection of the weakness of the U.S.A. relative to the power of the British empire; but, the most persistent of such outside influences, up to the present moment, has been a powerful residue of the financial power of the British East India Company's ostensibly wealthy influences such as those of the Boston Vault and New York's Wall Street, within the U.S. financial establishment itself.

Presently, the time has come, under President Barack Obama, at which there is a chance to break the British imperialist grip on the internal affairs of the U.S.A. The four crucial steps which I have indicated above, would be sufficient to put that achievement within our reach. If the U.S. succeeded in effecting that achievement, the opportunities for the improvement of the conditions in the world at large will have arrived, if we of the U.S.A. can muster the courage to bring that great benefit about.

A return, now, to the true economic principle of a credit-system presently still embodied in our Federal Constitution, that of that constitutional system of credit which had been first established in Massachusetts under its original royal charter, would be a change from the inherent, long-ranging ruin under a global, monetarist system, which is to be located, presently, in the contrast between a science of physical economy and the contrary, imperialist tradition which had reigned, and ruined, as the European maritime-imperialist tradition of imperialist regimes, that since such occasions as the death of Macedon's Alexander the Great.

So, once the 1933 Glass-Steagall law were put into force, again, the resulting cancellation of the U.S. government's obligation to "bail out" the financial waste-matter of monetarism, the cancellation of an immoral imposition of such forms of national indebtedness, would free the U.S. Government to muster trillions of fresh U.S. dollars for immediate recovery measures.

This revival of our nation's economy would free us to proceed to immediate steps of employing three to four millions of our most skilled, but presently largely unemployed labor, and also stimulate a related, much-needed economic recovery of our neighbors in Canada and Mexico. That first massive step of the initial economic recovery, would become the beginning of an implicitly global economic recovery of our prospective partners throughout much of the world: Franklin Roosevelt-style.

I explain that as follows.

Our American System

As I have emphasized, repeatedly, in earlier publications, that what U.S. Secretary of the Treasury Alexander Hamilton defined as "The American System of political-economy," is not only a fruit of the same constitutional system of physical principle fostered by leading economists such as, most notably, Alexander Hamilton, Henry C. Carey, and Presidents George Washington, John Quincy Adams, Abraham Lincoln, and Franklin Roosevelt. The needed American policy, as distinct from a European monetarist, and essentially imperialist system, was already the policy employed with brilliant success by the Massachusetts Bay Colony for as long as Britain had not violated the given charter of that colony. What had been done in Massachusetts, under that Seventeenth-century charter, was the actual birth of an American credit system inhering in the intention of our Federal Constitution.

In contrast, with but rare and brief exceptions, European nations which accept monetarism, as distinct from a system of national credit, have only rarely accepted such an economic reform as having inherently durable types of continued authority. This problem within Europe in particular, the problem of Europe from which American settlers had fled their native countries in a mixture of pride and despair, was that which passed, in law or practice, as premised on a deeply embedded, and usually victorious and traditional opinion in a law which provided the mechanisms of usurious practice of oligarchical policies of monetarist imperialisms, policies which had emerged from, among other sources, the Peloponnesian War. These had been prevalent as an expression of a maritime form of the practice of imperialism, as distinct, on this account, from the so-called "Asian model."

For example: the presently ruinous "Euro" system, was a "natural outgrowth" of the combination of British imperialism and the European oligarchical principle of monetarist practices, which have ruled, except for exceptions during relatively brief periods. Such relatively brief European exceptions include the development, during the 1877-1890 interval under the leading influence of Chancellor Bismarck; but, all too rarely, and, speaking in relative terms, briefly.

My own view on these matters of European traditions, does not begin within the bounds of the founding of the Massachusetts Bay colony itself. Christopher Columbus' zeal for actually discovering the shore of the land-mass which he then knew as early as 1480, existed at a certain distance across the Atlantic, had been made known to him through the circles of Cardinal Nicholas of Cusa and Cusa's own writings. This knowledge had been based, in turn, on the discovery of the size of the planet Earth as early as the discoveries by the great Eratosthenes.

The great scientist Nicholas of Cusa had warned that the oncoming decadence in European culture which followed the Venice-inspired, Ottoman conquest of Constantinople required contact with continents and peoples in places across the Earth's great oceans. Only thus, Cusa proposed, could the precious content which Europe had gained from that Renaissance known as the great ecumenical Council of Florence be preserved, which required reaching across great oceans to the continents beyond.

Henry VIII's judicial murder of Sir Thomas More sealed England's commitment to perpetual warfare, lasting until the 1648 Peace of Westphalia.

In that sense, all truly modern European culture has been premised upon two keystone writings of Cardinal Nicholas of Cusa: his ***Concordancia Catholica*** (the conception of the modern sovereign form of nation-state cultures), and Cusa's setting forth the conception of the sovereign form of modern nation-state society, as based on the conceptions which he presented in such works as his founding of modern science, as in ***De Docta Ignorantia***.

The same issue of the modern sovereign form of na-

tion-state cultures, underlies both the achievements and the inherent flaws of the tradition of parliamentary governments. Take into account the signal case of the deplorable actions taken under the influence of Venetian agents, such as Francesco Zorzi and Cardinal Pole, during the reign of England's Henry VIII.

Examine the case of Henry VIII's butchering of his great Chancellor, Sir Thomas More, by order of the Venetian party's agents such as Cromwell and Cardinal Pole.

The Roots of the British Empire

During the early days of Henry VIII's monarchy, a fragile religious peace reigned in an already troubled Europe, that despite what had already been the chronic Habsburg pollution of the royal marriage-beds of Spain. An already fragile peace among Spain, France, and England blocked the eruption of the general threat of an outbreak of general religious warfare which the Habsburg dynasty had set into motion with the 1492 expulsion of the Jews from Spain.[2]

The roles of the Venetian agents led by Henry VIII's devilish, Cusa-hating marriage-counsellor and Venetian intelligence operative, the cabalist Francesco Zorzi, and Henry's Thomas Cromwell, and Cardinal Pole, were crucial factors in the manipulations of the already fragile sanity of a failed Henry VIII whose lapses from sanity should remind us of such comparable cases of systemically "failed personalities," such as the Emperor Nero, Adolf Hitler, and of our own, Nero-like President, Barack Obama, and his associated, increasingly fragile cabal, now.

Amid the mass of butcheries unleashed by Henry VIII, the judicial murder of Sir Thomas More was the

---

2. Cf. the original, French version of Giuseppe Verdi's rendering of Friedrich Schiller's account of the relevant history, as in Verdi's ***Don Carlo***.

most crucial, since it was thus sealed, in More's blood, that England was commited to a state of perpetual religious warfare which would be, in fact, continued until the great 1648 Peace of Westphalia. Nonetheless, despite the urgency for future generations, of achieving that peace, the damage done by Henry VIII's role has crippled civilization's chances from that time to the present instant this report is written.

Of all the consequences of that religious warfare which continued until the 1648 Westphalian peace, subsequent history shows the worst to have been the way in which the Venetian party led by Paolo Sarpi cleared the way for that "Thirty Years War" between the twin Venetian factions of Sarpi and the Habsburg imperium which had combined roles to such net effect, that all of the major wars which the planet has subsequently suffered are an outcome of depraved poor Henry VIII's turn, which made possible, then, a "Venetian monetarist party" which continues, through its present British imperial puppet, to orchestrate all kindred evils, including two "World Wars" and the Hitler regime, up through the present day.

That pattern of developments which have occurred since the beginning of modern European civilization's history, since A.D. 1401, should be considered now as compelling us to focus on what has been for so many, the mysterious origins of the role of money in the entire sweep of ancient through modern European history since earlier than the time that the great Aeschylus composed his *Prometheus* trilogy.

That same issue, as viewed from the standpoint of reference to the case of Henry VIII, underlies the entirety of the tradition of parliamentary governments in Europe, such as that of Britain under the present, Sarpian form of the Anglo-Dutch, monarchical system of monetarist form of imperialist empire which was established under William of Orange and continued as a world empire in fact, up through the present day. Such has been the model conflict within European civilization, such as it has been, since Henry VIII's Venice-directed butchery of his own great Chancellor Sir Thomas More. Even European Presidential systems have the usually implied constitutional character of a parliamentary, rather than truly republican system, or a dictatorship. The "Bonapartist model," as typified by the regime of a creature soon turned into a Habsburg asset, Napoleon, and also his caricature, the British puppet Napoleon III, and also the so-called fascist sys-

tems of Europe and in often Habsburg-polluted Central and South America, have been refractions of the lack of that kind of truly republican conception which is typified by both the original, chartered Massachusetts Bay Colony and by the Federal Constitution of the United States.

That much said thus far, we conclude this prefatory portion of the report with the following points of clarification. For purpose of comparisons made with respect to matters of principle, consider the following.

From the standpoint of the realities of physical production and consumption, there is no competent notion of economic value in a system of money as such, except for the practical role of the use of money as a politically controlled form of a system of monies of respectively sovereign nation-states. That arrangement, once it were installed by a leading group among consenting nations, would be a money-system to be used, on principle, as an instrument for uttering public credit, in each case, by a specific, sovereign nation, as, for example, under a fixed-exchange-rate system, a system which U.S. President Franklin D. Roosevelt had written into the law of nations through the combination of the 1933 Glass-Steagall law and the 1944 Bretton Woods prescription for a fixed-exchange-rate system of international cooperation.

The international structure which FDR's law established, until the implicitly treasonous actual repeal, at that time, of the fixed-exchange-rate system during 1971-72. That fixed-exchange-rate arrangement, had been a structure also premised on the preceding, 1933, Glass-Steagall law. Once combined, as they had been under Franklin Roosevelt, the repeal of what had been a system of law which was now in the process of being destroyed, under President Nixon's administration, and would be actually destroyed for the remaining decades, by a British imperialist initiative launched in 1984 through the offices of British "Wall Street" tool J.P. Morgan's Alan Greenspan.

The repeal of those two U.S. laws, both Glass-Steagall and the fixed-exchange-rate system, on which the continued existence of an intended post-World War II monetary-economic stability had depended, cleared the way for U.S. Federal Reserve Chairman Alan Greenspan's "legalizing" of a massive corruption of the world's monetary systems, a corruption which relied on the premises of British launching of Lord Jacob Rothschild's imperialist Inter-Alpha Group (the so-called

The British launched an initiative in 1984 to destroy what remained of the FDR legacy, using J.P. Morgan bank's Alan Greenspan (shown here, left, with Robert Rubin on the right). The photo on the right shows the patriarch of the Morgan dynasty, J.P. Morgan, in 1914.

BRIC), which presently controls, directly, or indirectly, an estimated 70% of the world's imperialist international banking today.

The operation centered in what had been the awful folly of Jacob Rothschild's peculiar service to the avowedly imperial, British monarchy of Elizabeth II, has presently driven the planet as a whole to the immediate brink of a style of threatened Weimar-style hyperinflation which is presently consistent, on a global scale, with what was done to ruin the locality of Weimar Germany in 1923.

Unfortunately, in the history of a specifically European civilization in the aftermath of the fall of the rotted-out Persian empire, mere money, as distinct from the currency of a system of public credit of a nation, as under our own (often violated) Federal Constitution, has been abused, often, chiefly as an instrument of the species of inherent crimes against humanity which is otherwise known as usury. What has been imposed, thus, has been, chiefly, some form of maritime imperialism, that from about the time of the death of Alexander the Great, until the presently over-reaching, imperial power of the post-1971-72 British Empire, as that is now expressed by Lord Jacob Rothschild's 1971 creation, the British Empire's Inter-Alpha System and that system's Wall Street puppets.

We shall return to a further examination of this matter, after an indispensable examination of the principled, Asian roots of today's specifically European oligarchical models.

I. The Decline of Sumer as a Model

The best among the accessible sources for study of the origins of European monetary systems, and therefore of their "social diseases," has been the case of the decline and fall of that once-proud Sumer, which presents us with the image of a Sumerian culture of Indian-Ocean maritime characteristics in origin, which had initially prospered under what archeologists identify, descriptively, as its "bow-tenure" system. The effects of that culture's later decline and downfall, were shown, in significant degree, by the imprint left on the series of predominantly semitic cultures, such as that well-known case of Babylon, among the successors of the fallen Sumer. The same faults which sent the Sumerian culture into its ruined state, were often repeated among its successors in that Near East region.

Originally, Sumer had functioned under what is identified today as a "bow tenure" system. That is to emphasize, that the independent farmers, each family with its own management of its irrigated plot, held the plot under terms of its sharing of product with the warehousing provided under the reign of the relevant "priesthood." This social arrangement had been based on what relevant archeologists have termed a "bow tenure" system; the farmer was obliged to maintain and employ his weapons in defense of the society as a whole.

However, as happened in a rather similar fashion under the declining phase of such cases as the Baghdad Caliphate later, a muscular process of eroding the rights of the farmer, led to the inclination toward the ruinous salination of the farmers' plots, as ownership was then supplanted by share-cropping-like arrangements, which were succeeded by virtual slavery. I observed the aftermath of similar effects personally during a personal visit in Iraq during the early 1970s. The decline of what had been the great Caliphate of Charlemagne's time, was a clue to the kind of process I had examined up-river in Iraq during my visit.

That set of examples from what is now conventionally identified as once proud, "ancient Mesopotamia," which had, initially, prospered, should be employed as a bench-mark for study of the Middle East's successor, the subsequent, globally extended European history's chronic cycles of rise, decline, and fall under the monetary systems of the Mediterranean and Atlantic regions of the world, in particular. Like the present system of the essentially, Venetian, supranational, British empire and its European maritime predecessors, this process shows the effect of the substitution of monetarist systems for a system of relatively physical-economic values.

As I have noted, in opening this chapter, in the specific case of Sumer itself, the systemic stages of what became a fatal mode of physical-economic decline, was a decline which began with the spoiling of the "bow-tenure right" of the farmer, but also underwent moral and physical-economic decay through degradation of the farmer to a mere tenant, and, later, a virtual slave. Notably, the same Mesopotamian decadence ordered the process of the descent of the Baghdad Caliphate, from being, then, the world's center of assembled knowledge and progress, during the lifetime of Charlemagne's ally, the Caliph Haroun al-Raschid, into the decline of the Caliphate, under imported Turkic muscle,

into a decadence echoing the precedent of the decline of Sumer.

The pattern observed in the case of the decadence of Sumer, has been, as a matter of fact, the reigning, known, social-economic model there since that time. The difference between what was, in fact, the legendary "Asian model" of imperialism, and what the European model has now become under the domination of the European Union by subjugation to the present form of the British empire, is to be viewed as typified by the maritime culture's precedent of the Homeric view of the long, ruinous siege of Troy, and by the consequences of that as shown by the great dramatist Aeschylus.

This pattern, set by the decadence of Sumer, has been, as a matter of fact, the reigning social-economic model throughout most of this planet, since that time. The difference between the Asian model and what has become the present European model, lies essentially in the implications of the specifically maritime model of imperialism which was developed, initially, as a power within the region of the Mediterranean, as that is typified by reference to the Homeric view of the aftermath of the long, ruinous siege of Troy, and by the consequences of that as shown by the great dramatist Aeschylus.

This pattern in history, which can be studied in the case of the repeated declines within ancient Mesopotamia, was repeated under the Mediterranean maritime cultures which superseded the Asian model, as since the effect of the Peloponnesian War in the Mediterranean, and in the rise of the form of the Venetian maritime empire from the decaying corpse of Byzantium, as, also, in the rise of that maritime form of international usury which has become known as the British empire of today.

About 1492, the Venetian system of imperialism underwent a crucially significant strategic modification, as the leading edge of world maritime power shifted from the Mediterranean, into the Atlantic. In that process, the shift to the Atlantic, from the Mediterranean, assumed the form of the struggle for maritime supremacy among the Iberian peninsula, France, and those Anglo-Dutch maritime interests which were to be consolidated by the victory of the Anglo-Dutch maritime-imperial interests in the "Seven Years War," at the February 1763 Peace of Paris.

What did not change significantly with that shift from the Mediterranean to the Atlantic, was the essential role acquired by Venice. Venice, once established as

Creative Commons/M. Lubinski

Sumerian civilization spanned the 26th through 23rd centuries B.C.. Shown are ruins of the Sumerian city of Ur, in southern Iraq. In the distance is the reconstructed facade of the Great Ziggurat of Ur.

The Trojan War, the subject of Homer's Iliad, is believed to have occurred in the 12th Century B.C. Shown is a scene from the Homeric epic on an Attic amphora, ca. 520 B.C.

The Pelopponesian War (431-404 B.C.) consolidated the forces of usury and monetarism in the Greek world. A scene from that war is pictured here on an Attic amphora.

a power a little more than a millennium ago, remained the center of the organization of monetary power, while the outer husk of monetarist power, the Anglo-Dutch maritime interest, became the political and military capital of the increasingly global operations of the empire itself. Venice has never actually given up that role; it simply transferred some of its functions to the newly constituted London branch, all as a part of the adjustment to the shift from the Mediterranean to the Atlantic field of leading action.

The "Seven Years War," as Chancellor Bismarck emphasized during the British run-up for World War I, has remained the underlying strategic model for the maintenance of British imperialism since that time, as the case of two "World Wars" illustrates the point.

This chronic pattern among monetarist systems, is rooted, systemically, in such reductionist (e.g., "zero-technological growth") systems echoing Aeschylus' identification of the brutish Zeus's tyranny, as in the *Prometheus* trilogy, such as the pro-genocidal policy of British Prince Philip's pro-genocidal World Wildlife Fund (WWF) today. This legacy of "zero-growth" policy, as portrayed by the *Prometheus* trilogy, had been continued by such pro-genocidal, "zero population-growth" presumptions as those of the fellow-travelers of that systemic evil of an Aristotle who was later condemned by the associate of the Christian Apostle Peter, Philo of Alexandria. Philo attacked the legacy of Aristotle on precisely this issue. He attacked Aristotle's

dogma on its curious premise, of insisting that the Creator had ceased to be creative once the initial launching of an allegedly fixed organization of the universe had been consolidated.[3]

The Aristotelean model was superseded, in terms of forms of political systems, during the course of the European 1492-1648 religious warfare. This occurred by the interventions launched against the failed Council of Trent by the frankly satanic Paolo Sarpi, who is otherwise known as the virtual father of modern European liberalism. That is to emphasize the point, that, whereas, the Aristotelean legacy, as typified by such among its products as the *a-priori* presumptions of Euclidean geometry, had prescribed a "zero technological growth" model, Sarpi's systemic presumptions, which are presently familiar as the British imperialist philosophy of such avowed enemies of the United States of America as Lord Shelburne's Adam Smith and Jeremy Bentham, promote what amounts to the pro-genocidal "chaos theories" inherent in that mathematics of Bertrand Russell which is hostile to any actually physical scientific principles.

---

3. Silly Isaac Newton's "clock-winder" nonsense was an echo not only of Aristotle on this point, but also both the Satan-like figures of the Olympian Zeus of Aeschylus' *Prometheus Trilogy* and the "God is dead" slogan of Friedrich Nietzsche, and also such followers of Nietzsche, as not only Prince Philip, but, also, the satanic inclinations of such followers of Nietzschean "creative destructionists" Sombart and Schumpeter as President Obama's Larry Summers.

Prometheus Bound

The pattern, so described, as expressed as the fatal legacy of Sumer and similar social models of decadence, is typified for the cases of European and other later histories by the topic of Aeschylus's **Prometheus** and, also, such modern cases as the policies of Prince Philip's pro-genocidal World Wildlife Fund and its embedded, "anti-growth" cult of what is called, euphemistically, "environmentalism." This "anti-growth" cult is typified in its systemic features today as the doctrine of the most evil men of the Twentieth Century, Bertrand Russell and his crony H.G. Wells. The cult-doctrine of those characters and their followers in this view was not really a result of their fear that the world would be over-populated by people, but their fear that the people might not accept the standard of relative stupidity which had been assigned to them by the rulers of the British empire. That was the same issue treated by Aeschylus' **Prometheus Bound**.

The intrinsically fraudulent, British "Malthusian" ideology expressed by Britain's Prince Philip and his World Wildlife Fund, is essentially a product of the fear among ancient through modern oligarchies, that the general population of nations might become too intelligent to put up with being treated as virtual cattle under the reign of oligarchs. This is the issue addressed by Aeschylus' **Prometheus** trilogy, as expressed later as the so-called "oligarchical principle" prescribed, jointly by Macedon's Prince Philip and the Achaemenid empire, their proposal for what had been intended as a joint system of implicitly world-wide permanent oligarchical rule. This was the principle of hatred against the image of Prometheus which was expressed by Aristotle at that time. This is the principle of oligarchical rule which underlies the *a-prioristic* presumptions of Aristotle's follower Euclid. This is also the doctrine of "zero growth" which permeates such mid-Nineteenth-century ideologies as that of Rudolf Clausius and the followers of the cult of "the second law of thermodynamics" generally, up to the present day. Hence, the "zero-growth" cult of the devotees of Prince Philip's World Wildlife Fund. Hence, the "creative destruction" cult of such pro-fascist mentalities as Nietzsche, Sombart, Schumpeter, and President Obama's Larry Summers.

In that light, consider the practical alternative to the

Mongol ruler Hulaku Khan's army attacking Baghdad, the heart of the Abbasid Caliphate, in 1258 A.D. The city was completely destroyed, up to 1 million people killed, and the Golden Age of Islam brought to a close.

modern fascist notion of a "danger of over-population."

The known demographic patterns of trends of increase of the potential relative population-density, reflect the absolute distinction of the human being from all lower forms of life. In other words, the key to this point is expressed by the great Academician V.I. Vernadsky's rigorously scientific distinction of human populations (the noösphere) from the biosphere.

That is to say, that the human species-type is distinguished uniquely from all lower forms of life by our species' potential for *willful creation of* discovered universal physical principles, by means of which the potential relative population-density of the human species is *willfully* increased. All living processes do, admittedly, express a drive for *de facto* innovation and improvement of types of species from relatively lower, to higher qualities; but, only human beings are capable of

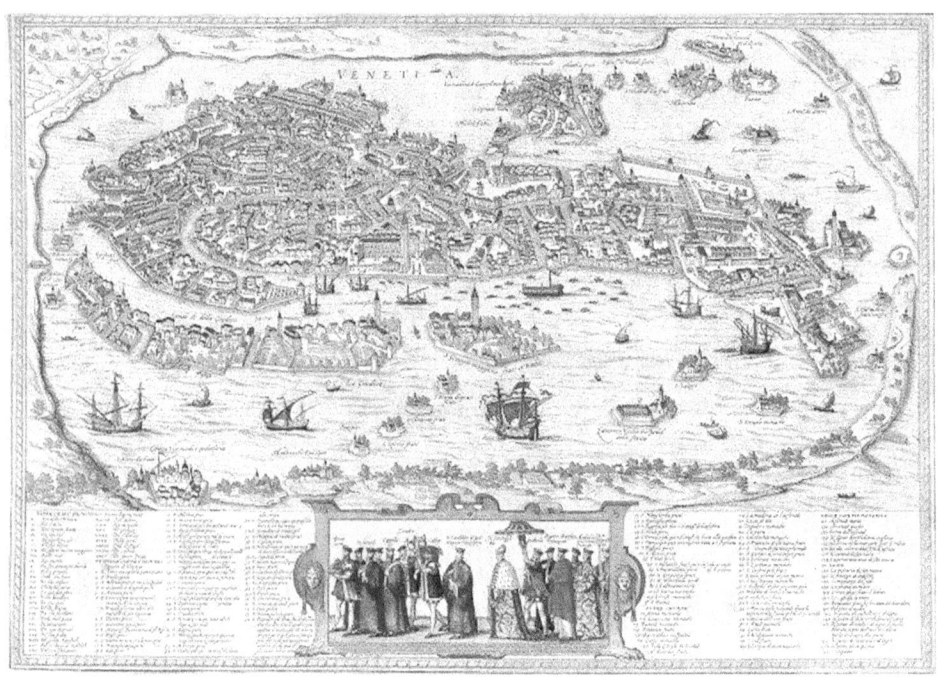

With the shift of power from the Mediterranean to the Atlantic, Venice remained the center of monetary power, while transferring some of its functions to London. Engraving of Venice by G. Braun and F. Hogenburg, 1565.

producing such anti-Aristotelean, "Promethean" effects as a creative act of willful knowledge of discovered principles, a kind of progress which is expressed in the mass as human voluntary progress through willful discovery of higher principles of action.

The general, willful advance in the potential relative population density of relevant cultures of the human species, is expressed generally as cultural changes associated with qualitatively improved means of sustaining a growing human population at a higher level of standard of living and life-expectancy through the fruits of cultural and scientific progress. The relevant forms of cultural progress are expressed as both discoveries of physical-scientific principles and as what are properly considered as advances in production of higher orders of cultural progress. The clearer notion of this modern notion of progress, is associated, most emphatically, with the legacy of the Florentine Renaissance's Filippo Brunelleschi and by Nicholas of Cusa and such among his followers in both science and Classical artistic composition as Leonardo da Vinci, Johannes Kepler, Gottfried Leibniz, and Johann Sebastian Bach. In fact, the creative powers of the human mind are to be associated with those aspects of mental function which are to be associated, specifically, with Classical modes of artistic composition, which are, in turn, associated with the creative powers of the developed individual mind's imagination, as the case of skilled amateur violinist Albert Einstein illustrates that connection.

The known, historical progress of combined scientific and Classical artistic culture in the history of European civilization, is to be correlated with such qualitative steps of progress as the development, under the leadership of Charlemagne, of the riparian systems developed under his leadership in statecraft. The progress in the potential for general advances in the physical conditions of human life, is expressed as leaps in potential typified by such cases as the addition of riparian development within Europe, as in the case of the reign of Charlemagne, to the already established maritime systems. The later development of the trans-continental railway system, is a comparable addition. The development of the use of nuclear and thermonuclear power, adds a still higher platform for the advancement of human potential population-density and of human culture generally. Mankind now awaits the conquest of nearby Solar space. Similarly, the work of my associates and I has revived the quasi-dormant intention to develop a leap in North American population-potential in the form of the implementation of the proposed North American Water and Power Alliance (NAWAPA), a development which can, and must be replicated in Eurasia and elsewhere. The next leap is into nearby Solar space: what has been named as "the extra-terrestrial imperative."

However, up to the present time, the progress in the conditions of life of the generality of the human species, has been a grudging progress, but a persisting impulse even in times when progress has been denied, or has suffered even catastrophic reversals imposed by the "environmentalists," instead. The great fear of the ruling oligarchies, such as we witness in the case of Britain's Prince Philip presently, has been that a people becoming "un-stupid" can not be treated as virtually often-overstuffed cattle. Hence, the theme of Aeschylus' *Prometheus* trilogy. Hence the plague known as Euclidean geometry.

II. Sarpi's Ockhamite Rule

That pattern in European history which is to be traced from the recurring cultural catastrophes in near-Asia, to the rise of the European society which followed the defeat of the Persian Empire by the forces under the command of Alexander the Great, was of the form of the rise to supremacy of a series of maritime cultures traced to what is efficiently identified as the Olympian model. The more than two past centuries, since 1763, which is represented by the domination of the planet by the British empire (initially, Lord Shelburne's British East India Company), corresponds to a new cultural phenomenon, a shift from the medieval European model of the followers of the cult of Aristotle, a shift to a new imperial cult, a shift embedded in the followers of the modern British cult of Paolo Sarpi.

It might appear to some, that the system of imperial maritime tyranny associated with the Sarpi legacy of the Thirty Years War period, could be considered a "capitalist" sort of post-Renaissance extrapolation of the medieval Aristotelean tyrannies. In fact, not only was Sarpi's system a systemically novel one at that time, but it was developed by Sarpi and his followers, such as his lackey Galileo, this as a reaction to the great threat to oligarchism typified then by the strategist Nicolò Machiavelli and the great scientist Johannes Kepler, but, more importantly, it was a reaction to the perceived threat of the modern science launched by such central figures of the Florentine Renaissance as Filippo Brunelleschi and Cardinal Nicholas of Cusa. It had been Cusa's founding of a systemically modern science, as typified by both his pioneering in the cause of the modern sovereign nation-state, *Concordancia Catholica*, and of modern science, *De Docta Ignorantia*, which represented the essential threat to the power of the Venice-centered, Sixteenth-century oligarchical forces. It was the failure of the Habsburgs and also their Inquisition, to defeat the legacy of the modern nation-state and its science by means of the great religious warfare launched by that Inquisition of 1492-1648, which brought about the defeat of the initial efforts to crush modern civilization through religious warfare, which had opened the gates, so to speak, for the emergence of Paolo Sarpi as leader of a new form of oligarchical tyranny, and continued warfare, a new tyranny which was specifically designed to counter the threat of the modern science by a system of sovereign nation-states which had been premised upon the discoveries launched by, chiefly, the influence of Cusa.

The then old, now failed, Aristotelean system, had opposed the Classical Greek science of such as Archytas and his friend Plato by, chiefly, the methods associated with Aristotle's system of intended, "virtually zero scientific progress." The cultural and scientific revolution led by Cusa outflanked the Aristotelean method, by re-establishing what was to become a modern principle of progress in the human condition through the discovery of universal physical principles. Under the influence of Cusa's policies, the resistance to the Habsburg butchers represented a new kind of strategic method, one which became associated with the name of Machiavelli, which the Aristotelean tradition was, inherently, poorly equipped to defeat.

So, the belabored Council of Trent had proven itself to be a strategic failure. The European oligarchy found an alternative in the utterly irrationalist doctrines of a resurrected medieval figure, William of Ockham ("Occam"). Sarpi's putatively Ockhamite dogma allowed innovations, even philosophically wild concoctions such as the black-magic specialist Isaac Newton, but always denied the existence of reason. The cult associated with the name of a half-witted black-magic specialist, nonetheless served the purposes of such duped followers of not only Sarpi and his Galileo, but also of the Abbé Antonio S. Conti whose role has proven to be that of the principal hand behind the duped followers of the anti-Leibniz cult. That is the cult of Sarpian Liberalism which has been largely continued up to the present day of the modern mathematical reductionists of associations such as Bertrand Russell's followers of the pseudo-scientific cult of the International Association for Applied Systems Analysis (IIASA) and IIASA's companion cult, the so-called Club of Rome.

Prince Philip and his late co-conspirator Prince Bernhard have followed Russell in their roles as the founders of the radically homicidal policies of the World Wildlife Fund (WWF), an association which is currently dedicated to a rapid reduction of the world's population to not more than two billions living persons. This genocidal motive is presented under the cloak of a deception called "environmentalism," a ruse for luring the WWF's duped fanatics into choosing a policy of what is in fact a more radical genocide than that intended by Adolf Hitler, all in the name of defending the lives of all sorts of usually four-legged, sub-human varieties of living specimens, against being, allegedly, crushed under the heel of alleged human "over-population." All of which is actually nothing other than the combined impoverishment of peoples and a Malthusian reduction of the human population on a scale fit to dwarf the evil imagination of Adolf Hitler's mass-murderers.

Such are exactly the pro-genocidal policies, in effect, of the current U.S.A.'s Barack Obama administration.

The United States, and also western and central Europe, are currently, immediately confronted with two general options. One is to resume science-driven technological progress, thus meeting the present urgent requirements of defending a healthy, and improved environment, or, going to the contrary extremes of imposing a mass-murderous practice of greatly increased death-rates through a murderous combination of "health-care reforms" and population reduction through mass impoverishment and destruction of efforts at net technological progress.

In fact, we have available presently, the means both to improve health-care standards for a growing population, and provide a greatly improved set of conditions for the enjoyment of a productive life generally. The only precondition for carrying out such policies, is accelerated support for technologically improved, and accelerated productivity, as to be accomplished through aid of science-driven progress. Yet, especially since the U.S. Presidency of Theodore Roosevelt, what may be fairly identified as the roots of the contemporary Wall Street-oriented parasitical class, have frequently worked in the direction of the wicked "environmentalist" schemes of the co-thinkers of Theodore Roosevelt, Prince Philip, and Prince Bernhard, all in the name of the great lie known as "defending the environment."

Sumer Again

Similarly, looking back to the case of the decline of Sumer, the systematic stages of what became the fatal mode of physical-economic decline there, began with the spoiling of the "bow tenure" right of the farmer, the

Sarpi's Lies

Venetian agent Paolo Sarpi (1552-1623) "wrote his doctrine for the proverbial suckers, not for himself," LaRouche writes.

Sarpi maintained that universals have no existence whatsoever; what do exist are objects perceived by the senses.

Sarpi's advice: "Do not follow opinion that wears the title of truth, but rather opinion that wears the title of pleasure or usefulness."

The wise man, according to Sarpi, "recognizes that his efforts at obtaining knowledge always come up against the infinite, and, knowing this is beyond his grasp, he stops and comes to no final decision on any matter, deciding to live according to the day-to-day appearance of things and, in public, support those beliefs which are commonly held. . . .

"The end of man, as of every other living creature, is to live . . . simply live in the here and now."

farmer's degradation to the status of a hired servant, and, later, a virtual slave. The typically oligarchical impulse for the degradation of the irrigation systems and fertility of the plots, which were the effects of the decline in the social status of the population generally, led then, and repeated in many cases later, to the fall of that civilization. So, the decline of the Baghdad Caliphate, later, typified the same type of process, of moral decay mixed with physical bankruptcy of the society as a whole.

Two points are to be made here on that account.

First, what is deemed to have been the relatively depleted "natural resources" on which the society had depended is the threat of doom for any society which does not effect sufficient rates of technological advance in the productive power of labor to off-set the systemic depletion of the relatively richest concentrations of such resources. Sooner, or later, that depletion requires the remedy of a revolution in basic economic infrastructure, even new principles of science. No "steady state" for a society which attempted to rely upon a fixed technology is possible.

The predecessor of Obamacare: euthanasia in Nazi Germany. More than 10,000 people with disabilities were killed at Hadamar Hospital, shown here, in 1941.

FDR Library

President Franklin D. Roosevelt's greeting to a young polio patient at Warm Springs, Ga., expresses the American System approach to health care: Make them well, don't kill them off!

Creative Commons/Steve Rhodes

A protest against health-care budget cuts in California, June 2009. California led the way for what has become the national Obamacare program.

Second, that same challenge must be examined in terms of what are three components of the requirements which a successful society requires. The first of these is "basic economic infrastructure," as this is best typified at this time by the crucial importance of implementation of the North American NAWAPA program as a leading feature of those nations' basic economic infrastructure. The second, is the qualitative advance of the technology used for overcoming the depletion of used resources of production. This includes the requirement of an increase of the energy-flux density of the sources of power available for both infrastructure and production and transport of goods. The technological advances required, including the general increase of the energy-flux density available and applied for both infrastructure and production, are essentially qualitative, rather than merely quantitative. The intellectual development of the society becomes of increasing importance as the capital-intensity of required levels of production must be maintained. Here, the intellectual life of the population becomes an increasingly important factor of costs of production and maintenance of the society.

The Ockhamite system, as typified by the case for the British economy, suffers from a systemic conflict between meeting the challenge of attrition, while keeping the population sufficiently relatively stupefied, culturally, that for the purpose of preventing the population from shucking off the burden of a reigning, essentially parasitical oligarchy. At the point that knowledge becomes the surge of freedom from oligarchical overlordship, the oligarchical society, such as Britain today, faces a most challenging contradiction. It can not maintain the emphasis on keeping a population relatively stupefied, and also meeting the challenge of increasingly urgent science-driven, capital-intensive requirements.

The case of IIASA is an excellent illustration of the kinds of effects prompted by that challenge.

Look back to the impact of the rise of modern physical chemistries which put an increasing premium on those aspects of progress in physical chemistry which, like the work of Louis Pasteur and Max Planck, and, then also V.I. Vernadsky, require increasing emphasis on the products of the genius of Bernhard Riemann. Into the fray between competent science and the fears of the British and like oligarchies, we find the case of Bertrand Russell. The more simple-minded opposition to science from the likes of Ernst Mach, is no longer sufficient; the more drastic obscenities of a Bertrand

EIRNS/Claudio Celani

Russell send Twentieth-century science into an increasingly intense conflict between mere mathematics and the increasingly Riemannian sophistication of what has been predominantly a Riemannian physical chemistry since Louis Pasteur, Dmitri Mendeleyev, Max Planck, William Draper Harkins, Albert Einstein, and Academician V.I. Vernadsky.

The British and kindred oligarchies of science, since the roles of the so-called mathematical physics of David Hilbert et al., are gripped by the challenge of keeping up with the progress and related demands of honest scientific achievements, and the danger to the oligarchical interest which an honest scientific practice represents, Hence, the rather crucial significance of Russell's brutish political role in producing a *Principia Mathematica*, and kindred trappings of pseudo-science, combined with attempting to use mere mathematics in a fashion applied by the Russell circles in the 1920s Solvay conferences. David Hilbert was not utopian enough! More drastically radical measures launched by the academic rabble of the Bertrand Russell cult were demanded.

The result of the upsurge of Russell and his like during the period of the 1920s Solvay conferences, has been, notably, the drive into the depths of absurdity represented by the "Cambridge systems analysis" and such of its by-products as the IIASA "brainwashing" enterprise in sterile, merely mathematical computations. A mere, lunatic mathematics of bad, actually unpayable gambling debts, is devouring, and has nearly consumed what might appear to be the real universe, while the actual production of real wealth is being closed down for no reason as much as the shift from emphasis on a physical science, rooted in crucial experimental progress in experimental physical science, to a sterile sort of merely mathematical one.

The "John Law bubble"-like character of the present insanity associated with the money systems of the planet, has virtually taken over the economy. The point has been reached, at which either most of the nominal money-wealth of the world is simply cancelled, or society itself will be virtually cancelled in another of the great waves of genocidal "new dark ages."

There are two issues posed in this fashion.

First, money as such can no longer be regarded as representing an intrinsic measure of economic value. Only money as an expression of uttered national credit, rather than a content of value, can survive. Economic value exists only in what can be defined as an expression of efficiently physical value, as in the increase of the potential relative population-density of society. Money becomes, thus, the promise of the sovereign nation-state to produce something of intrinsically new efficient values of that quality to society. Henceforth, the use of money must be restricted to the authority of sovereign government to utter such credit for such intended ends.

It happens, then, that the investment in what I have classed as a proper definition of basic economic infrastructure, represents the chief item of purchase and consumption in a modern society. This is the platform on which the existence of other forms of value depend for their existence. Professionals who reject such tasks, whatever their nominal profession, have proven themselves consistent failures in the domain of the necessary science of physical, rather than monetarist economy.

Take the current case of the projected building of the NAWAPA system as a most relevant example.

The NAWAPA Revolution

NAWAPA, when installed will be the greatest work of infrastructure-building existing on this planet thus far. Nonetheless, it will do much more than merely pay for itself. It represents the greatest gain in the productive value of the relevant territory in the history of mankind to date. Moreover, it will promote supplements in territories on other continents which will become integral with the functions of NAWAPA, and will provide a greater rate of gain in the productive powers of labor, and per unit of relevant territory, than any yet seen on this planet.

Consider the following illustration.

Ordinarily, the idea of "productive" is associated with the output of labor by production. That is an honest mistake in judgment. The fact of the matter is, that the precondition for the rise of cultures to revolutionary changes to higher qualities of regions of sustainable, potential relative population-density, depends on virtual leaps in potential relative, human population-density which, in turn, require a higher quality of physical-cultural "platform" within which to operate. Such platforms include the discoveries in astronomy on which trans-oceanic maritime cultures depend. They include the addition of the inland riparian cultures, featuring canal-systems linked to principal rivers. They include most extensive systems of transport, such as good quality of highway systems, and then continental railway systems. They include advances in the cultural level of forms of power, from relatively lower, to higher effective energy-flux-densities of the form of power employed.

So, presently, the preconditions for the next great upward leap in the world's economy, now depend not only upon nuclear and thermonuclear power, as superseding types of qualitatively lower ranges of energy-flux-densities. They require a general upgrading of the methods of management of the planet, as this revolution is typified by the NAWAPA design.

It is the great advances in basic economic infrastructure which NAWAPA presently exemplifies, which constitute the platforms on which the potential for increase of relative potential population-density and quality of individual human life depend. In other words, the level of achievable productivity depends upon raising the "platform," through revolutions in infrastructure, on which successful general advances in potential relative population-densities depend. Without those advances in basic economic infrastructure, merely particular technological progress locally applied will fail in attempted performance of the truly vital mission of physical-economic program, failing for lack of the progress in advancement of the quality of the infrastructural platform on which the success of the society as a whole depends.

III. The Factor of Creativity

The time has now come, here, to repeat, in a fuller fashion, a point of great importance, to which I have had occasion to report upon a number of similarly relevant settings.

The most significant advance in modern physical science since the discoveries of Filippo Brunelleschi, Nicholas of Cusa, Leonardo da Vinci, et al., was the uniquely original discovery of the principle of universal gravitation by Johannes Kepler. As Albert Einstein emphasized, the crucial discovery bearing on the system of the universe as a whole, was the discovery by Kepler which implicitly defined our universe as *finite, but, yet, unbounded.*

No reductionist, whether of the variety of Aristotle, nor the followers of Sarpi, has ever shown insight into understanding of the great principles of modern physical science which such geniuses as Leibniz and Bernhard Riemann owed to the crucial element of method underlying Kepler's discovery of the universal principle of gravitation. The case of Helen Keller supplies a delicious choice of hint as to how that elementary discovery by Kepler came into being.

The great problem of science which remains largely, one must say, stubbornly unsolved in the usual modern classroom or laboratory, lies in the usual failure to see the obviously ironical significance of human sense-perception. Here, we encounter the greatest of all the crucial principles of science. It is a certain general failure to understand the practical meaning of scientific qualities of creativity, among even scientifically educated professionals, which is still, today, the usual, qualitative barrier to be conquered along the pathway of general scientific and cultural progress in general.

In my earlier publications of recent years, I have concentrated considerable, repeated effort in my attempts to bring clarity to the discussion of that obstacle and its meaning. It is a subject of great relevance in this present location. This problem, however challenging it may be, is nonetheless of an elementary, although crucial nature for all scientific work which treats elementary principles of observation. The argument which I have repeatedly employed on this account, runs as follows.

I now repeat an argument which I have employed repeatedly in earlier occasions.

Imagine that you are the commander of a space ship, but one without any directly sensory observation of the

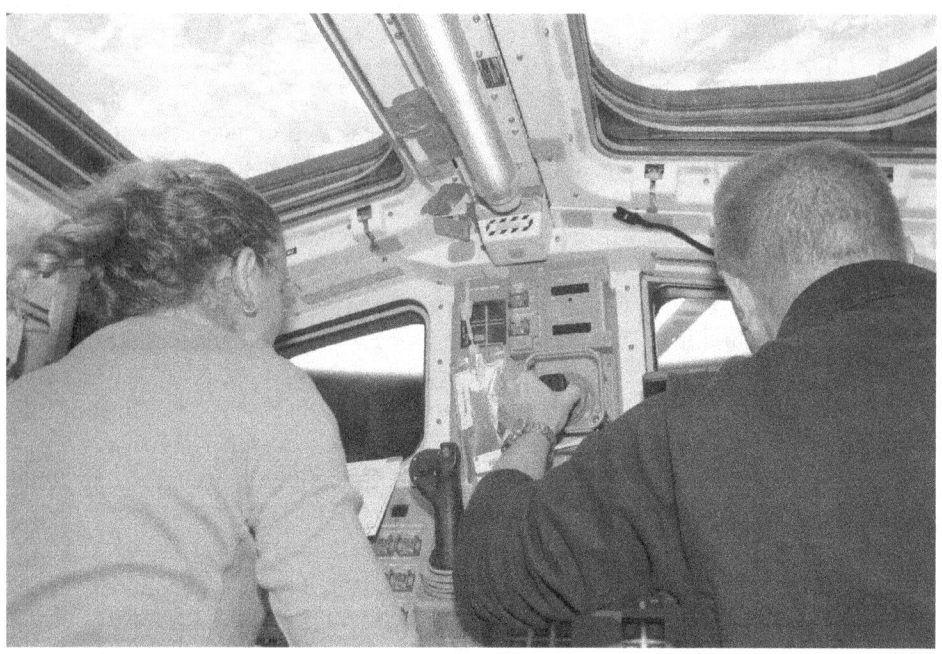

The commander of a space ship cannot rely on the essential unreality of sensual inputs concerning his or her surroundings, but must creatively use an array of even paradoxical inputs to find the way. Shown: Astronaut Julie Payette and pilot Doug Hurley on the Space Shuttle Endeavor, July 29, 2009.

contrast of the view of the Solar System provided by the contradictory notion of vision, when compared with a sense of the harmonics displayed by the patterns among the planetary orbits. Thus, neither of those two sensibilities, defined the principle of gravitation; only the ironically contradictory juxtaposition of the two views, provided Kepler access to the actual principle commonly underlying the experience of the sets of the two contrasted qualities of assumed sense-perceptual developments.

Of crucial importance for this argument, is that our example presumes acting upon what is often regarded as "the empty space" lying between the planetary orbits. There is no empty space, in fact. That imputed "space" is chock-full of cosmic radiation.

outside medium through which you are traveling. Your essential resources for sensing the performance of your function as a pilot, are scientific instruments which, like the human sense-perceptions, do not present you with the real space through which your craft is traveling, but merely the equivalent of meter-readings on the wall of your cabin. Just as a sea captain might do, you must rely on your understanding of the essential unreality of the common reading of each of your senses, and do this to such effect that you master the fact of the mutual contradictoriness of several kinds of instruments on which you must rely for the purpose of adducing the reality which none among the available sensory instruments actually presents.

The paradoxical character of the array of human senses which are, always, in fact, in immediate contradiction with one another, must lead you, as a navigator, to a discovery of a fact which none of your senses, by itself, could accomplish. You are confronted with a challenge akin to that which Johannes Kepler faced in the course of his discovery of a principle of universal gravitation which no particular sense-organ could define on its own account.

Kepler's actual, and uniquely original discovery of the principle of gravitation, relied upon the paradoxical

The more crucial, and deeper point illustrated by that case, is the fact that reality as such, does not correspond to mere sense-perception as such. After all, the allegedly "sensed" empty space, does not actually exist. Thus, it is demonstrated, that the human mind is not a product of sense-perception; but, rather, the exact opposite. So, when we employ instruments to gain a reflection of those aspects of experience which are specific to the experience of the domain of the very large, or very small, which the concluding section of Bernhard Riemann's 1854 habilitation dissertation had already located as beyond the reach of literal sense-perception, we have entered into a higher domain of the universe, beyond simple sense-perception; our experience with such discoveries, is then reflected to us as a domain of scientific discovery beyond the imagination of ordinary sense-perception.

Yet, this is a domain of reality, nonetheless. The crucial, if paradoxical fact of the matter is, that we are not creatures defined by our senses; we are higher beings, with a much higher order of creative potential than our mere, conventional notions of our senses would suggest. Our minds, which are our true selves, are of a higher form of existence than the literal readings of mere sense-perception might suggest.

The apparent ontological paradox which that evidence implies, defines the notion of any existing universal physical principle, and does so in terms coherent with the ontological paradox which I have just implied in these terms of reference. Reality is then located for us outside those mere sense-perceptions which are but shadows cast by that unsensed, but nonetheless unavoidable reality of our existence. Those realities are what are properly recognized as being expressions of the reality beyond the direct reach of those mere shadows which are the sense-experiences. Such is the seemingly paradoxical nature of any valid discovery of a universal physical principle.

Thus, neither the Aristoteleans, nor the empiricists could have attained any competent insight into the reality of that universe which we inhabit. That relationship which I have just so described, points to those powers of the creative imagination which we should associate with both scientific discovery of true principles of the universe and the modes of Classical artistic composition. All competent proofs of any principle belong to that domain of the imagination. So Classical artistic composition of the domain of the unseen, pre-figures valid scientific insight into the discovery of physically efficient realities.

Hence, the Problem!

Now, here, from the vantage-point of these immediately preceding considerations, the competent notion of national and related economic credit, as in, and among national economies, is to be derived from the considerations so presented in this chapter thus far. As in the concluding, third section of Bernhard Riemann's 1854 habilitation dissertation, any physically real notion of the economic quality of credit should be defined as: reasonable confidence in what we must observe that we must discover, as a matter of principle, that we have the power to cause to happen, considering matters in the terms of reference which I have employed in this present chapter of my report, thus far. The most crucial aspect of this is presented as the power to cause to happen what has never been known to have been done before. Such is the role of the principle of scientific foresight premised on a rigorously defined view of the principle of hypothesis considered by Riemann, as by such as Plato before him.

Compare the exemplary cases of Archytas' duplication of the cube, and Eratosthenes' measurement of the estimated size of the Earth; do so, in the latter case, by means of the shadows cast by the Sun. Or, consider the proofs developed by Academician V.I. Vernadsky for the categories of the abiotic, biotic, and human cognitive domains of practice. Then, examine, rigorously, the related notion of the role of metaphor in defining a demonstrable notion of a universal principle, as for the case of John Keats' *Ode on a Grecian Urn*. *Metaphor may thus be considered as the essence of reality.*

Kindred Implications

Once we have reflected upon the points just listed above: why should we be so simple-minded as to presume that our experience of the world outside of our skins should be limited to the domain of a naive view of the work of the given human senses? Must we not, rather, regard the popular faith in such sensory experiences as merely a sampling from a much larger array of comparably knowable modes of experience?

Is it, perhaps, our tendency to that simplistic notion of "self-evident" particles of matter which conventional notions of simple sense-certainty suggest to us, which misleads us into overlooking the immense range of cosmic radiation, including that which is, or is not compatible with the requirements of life in general, or human life in particular? After we have conceded that such radiation can not be overlooked in considering the effects to which we are subject, why should we exclude an innate potential for human beings' discovery of a conscious apprehension of such "additional channels" whose effects are potentially accessible as knowledgeable experiences equivalent to sense-perceptions in the ordinary, customary sense? Take the cases of more or less well-defined mass experiences which have manifest effects on the moods associated with conscious states of "awareness." Granted, there are doubtful cases, in which inductive judgments from ordinary sense-perceptual experiences are relevant; is that all? What of Rosa Luxemburg's remarkably apt perception of the phenomena of the "mass strike"?

Or, in the alternative, consider the experiences, such as those involving crucial-experimental tests of principle, which depend upon sensory experiences premised on instruments which reach outside the domains of ordinary sense-perceptions, as Bernhard Riemann emphasized this in the concluding section of his habilitation dissertation.

There can be no physically empty space! Suddenly,

with that thought, Riemann's warning against careless presumptions respecting the very large and very small, strike home.

To somewhat similar effect, what might be the ontological implication of the range of diseases which are more or less clearly associated with radiation, both as physical disorders of living processes, and also as cures? Once we have taken into account the fragility of the process of adducing sense-certainties from sensory experience alone, we are confronted with the problem of defining certainty in respect to the biological experiences as such, but, also, with more than strong hints that this also involves dimensions of communication, or potential forms of communication among living species existing outside the domain of so-called "conventional" experience of human communication. The certainty of such seemingly anomalous matters, such as those, remains as located in the fact that the human mind operates from outside, and absolutely "above" the domain of sense-perception as we have become accustomed to believe that we know it.

Suddenly, the true meaning of "cosmic radiation" strikes home, probably in the following way.

What, in terms of ontology, is the nature of the attributable "physical reality" of a discoverable, and demonstrable universal physical principle? None of that actually exists in either the teachings of Aristotle or the followers of Sarpi. Yet, only a liar could deny that the original discovery of universal gravitation was made by Johannes Kepler. The only persons who actually believe that Newton was a scientist, are merely acting as hysterics: they have been taught to believe, but not because they have valid supporting evidence for that belief that that is in evidence; they believe because they are frightened by the threat to their career, or something akin to that, which might strike them if they do not profess to believe, as if very sincerely, in certain things which may not actually exist. Yet, we are nonetheless able to demonstrate in practice, as I have already emphasized in this publication up to this point, that subsuming principles of the universe do exist outside the category of our sense-perceptions, and are unique.

Why do they believe such nonsense as sense-perception per se? Aeschylus knew the answer. Hence, his *Prometheus Bound*.

Think of the lists of discoveries of universal physical principles. Without discovery of such principles we were as miserable as mere beasts, and would render ourselves to being among the most pitiably helpless of them.

The Prometheus Myth

Consider a listing of an array of discoveries of proven universal physical principles, which exist as true principles only "outside" pure and simple sense-perceptions, even principles without which mankind would be just another mere beast. Consider the stubbornness, even the viciousness, with which many persons had reacted to reject such discoveries. Think of the results in such cases. What should we make of such historical evidence, in case after case?

That much considered: what must we make of the case of Aeschylus' Prometheus? What is that evidence from history, which shows such a factor has often been an historical fact? Point to examples of cases in which what had been proven to be a truly discovered, efficient principle, had yet been resisted, even forbidden. Take the case of the Aristotelean Euclid. It is a rather easy argument to demonstrate that the *a-priori* presumptions of Euclidean geometry do not actually exist as principles of practice in competent physical practice, as I, for example, had come to understand the principle involved already at the age of 14, simply by the prompting of my fascination with the reason for the "holes" in structural steel which I had studied at the Charlestown Navy Yard.

Think of the silliness of much of the discussion of the subject of a so-called "non-Euclidean" geometry during the course of the 19th Century, and even beyond that. Consider Carl F. Gauss' gingerly avoiding discussing the actual issue in the case of Jonas Bolyai, but also regard Gauss seated in sponsorship of his sometime protégé Bernhard Riemann as Riemann presented the case in the habilitation dissertation he delivered on that occasion.[4] Today, we know that Gauss employed principles of discovery of physical principle which we must acknowledge, as if retroactively, as expressing essential principles of work which we came to know only retroactively, even only mathematically, rather than as actually physical principles of experimental method. Gauss did this on numerous occasions, as he did in his letter in response to his friend, Jonas Bolyai's father. The idea that a deductive mathematics could never define a true physical principle, died very hard among the mathematicians in that and other instances.

Take the cases of two crucial principles of modern practice, that of nuclear power and that of chlorophyll. Consider the far worse than silly doctrines expressed by

---

4. The concluding, daringly ironical sentence of that habilitation dissertation, is stunning if one thinks about it retrospectively.

the proliferation of such worse than useless, even menacing types of substitutes for efficient selections of sources of power as windmills and solar panels. Compare the unavoidable amount of cost per calorie of each gimmick with that of nuclear power. What is expressed by the would-be Olympian Zeuses of today is demonstrated in fact to be a gigantic religious fraud, and, in fact, what is fairly viewed as being a Satanic sort of religion.

Behind the promotion of such monstrous frauds as that of windmills and solar panels is nothing different that what Aeschylus emphasized in the **Prometheus** trilogy. What these toys express, is not science, but very bad social theory—that in the sense of "bad" to be considered as bordering on the Satanic.

There is a relevant, somewhat misty, but nonetheless demonstrable case to be considered in coming to an understanding of the purely political principle behind the motives of those who, still today, wish to consider themselves the virtual representatives of gods of Olympus. The principle involved can be understood with help of some historical evidence.

Olympia & the Berbers

At some time after the beginning of the great melt of the last great glaciation of the northern regions of our planet, "people of the sea" appeared along the coasts of the Mediterranean. In the case of a people who received such mariners, we have the Berbers already long established there. The legend is that the concubine of a head of the mariner's party, called Olympia, induced her sons, among whom Zeus led the pack, to kill their mother's husband. Later, we find these Olympians styling themselves as "gods" reigning over the lower class of ordinary human beings, all as we have it from the Homeric **Iliad** and **Odyssey** and the retrospective view provided by playwright Aeschylus.

Thus, we have, from the Homeric sources and those of Aeschylus et al., a view of the composition of the ancient society of the Mediterranean as it appears to us from such sources as the Great Pyramid of Giza, and, afresh from the warring maritime forces of the Mediter-

wikipedia
The ancient "people of the sea" clashed with the Egytian dynasty of Ramses III in the 12th Century B.C. A scene from the north wall of Medinet Habu illustrates the Egyptian campaign against the Sea Peoples in what has come to be known as the Battle of the Delta.

ranean from about the Seventh Century B.C. We are enabled to untangle some of the accounts pertaining to these topics through a crucial aspect of the accounts associated with the physical-scientific doctrines of Sphaerics and the work of such as the Pythagoreans.

From these records and the like, we have a picture of a great struggle among leading forces in society, as only typified by the Plato vs. Aristotle accounts. Aristotle, who was actually a control agent and celebrated poisoner in the service of Macedon, typifies what is known from the history of such times, and later, as "the oligarchical principle" which Aeschylus' and other accounts associate with the oligarchical code of the Olympians.

No competent evidence exists in support of the presumption that those matters are merely stories. The differences in the manifest mental processes of the Pythagoreans and such as the followers of Aristotle, are of such a character that there can be no doubt but that such controversies correspond to a scientifically systemic form of conflict in matters of opposing systems which are definable as such in terms of scientific principles. Among the most significant categories of evidence bearing on this subject is that dated from the interval of the roles of Macedon under the succession of Philip of Macedon and Alexander the Great.

Out of the developments during that period, there was the attempt to define a world empire shared by two proposed partners, the Achaemenid Empire as the land power of Asia, and the maritime region associated with the Mediterranean. Under Philip of Macedon, this two-

Topkapi Palace Museum

Plato's enemy Aristotle, the celebrated poisoner of Macedon's Alexander the Great, typifies the oligarchical principle. Shown here are a coin with the image of Philip of Macedon (ca. 323 B.C.), and a drawing of Aristotle teaching geometry (13th-Century Turkish School).

empire system was to be a world empire constituted by a pact, known as the "oligarchical principle," between the two parties. This scheme was spoiled, for a time, by the accession of Alexander which occurred, as follows below, after a contentious period set off by the death of Philip.

The Achaemenid empire was destroyed by the victory of the forces led by Alexander in the great battle at Gaugamela. However, the intent to establish an empire based upon "the oligarchical principle," has persisted in that region to the present day. Presently, it is properly named the "British Empire." It is the legacy of what was known as the oligarchical order associated with the tradition of the Delphi cult of Apollo, an Apollo-Dionysos cult whose last famous high priest was the Roman Plutarch remembered by political illiterates still today as the author of the tendentious chronicle called "Plutarch's Lives of Famous Men."[5]

The importance of my immediately stated account of that historical summary here, is that the oligarchical principle traced from such reflections as the dramas of Aeschylus and their known precedents then, and still earlier, is a plainly embedded syndrome of the ascendant, specifically European maritime-cultural legacy presently. It is the same oligarchical principle of corruption of European society which prompted Cardinal Nicholas of Cusa to propose the launching of great voyages across the oceans in search of locations from which to build up the foundations of a society which would, subsequently, be free of Europe and the Medi-

terranean region.

Thus, the British empire which dominates Europe today, and the spill-over of that empire into the financial centers of Boston, New York, Chicago, and so on, inside the U.S.A., and reigning still over most of the nations of Central and South America, remains presently as the legacy of an agency based on that same oligarchical principle which Aeschylus' **Prometheus** trilogy identified for our strategic political edification today.

True creativity, as I have pointed out here, is the specific distinction of man from beast, whereas oligarchism persists, still today, and represents a beastly form of attempted reign by wittingly beastly tyrants who regard ordinary men and woman as virtually the cattle of an oligarchical system. The continuing struggle to secure the full independence of the United States under the conditions of the dominant role of a British oligarchical empire, is still today's great issue of the freedom of the creative powers innate to the culture of the human species.

The issue is, that if ordinary men and women are permitted to escape from the cultural manipulations of a reigning oligarchical system, the oligarchical system would die, hopefully forever.

What confronts us all just now, is an attempt to re-impose a frankly genocidal program typified by the legacies of Aristotle, or Paolo Sarpi, or their like, upon a human population which, considered in the large, requires forms of science-driven progress in the physical-productive powers of labor needed to sustain the present levels of population through advances in technology by means of which we are enabled to do better than merely supersede the effects of attrition.

At the same time, the motive of that oligarchy which is now still centered in the oligarchical rule over the globally extended monetary system defined by the British empire of Lord Shelburne's Adam Smith et al., is to prevent a new wave of science-driven progress in the productive powers of human labor, a progress which, by its very nature, would destroy the ability of the oli-

_____

5. The Apollo-Dionysos cult lives on as the expression of the oligarchical cult still to the present time.

garchical tradition to continue to enjoy its power to rule over the planet as a whole today. To that end, the British empire refurbished under what Lord Jacob Rothschild launched as the Inter-Alpha Group, beginning 1971, has embarked on the greatest wave of intended genocide against the great majority of the human species now. With the oligarchy of the world, that intention is the currently existential quality of hatred of the deeds and memory of such paragons as President Franklin Roosevelt.

As we of the U.S.A. used to write and publish, during the days of World War II: "Know your enemy!"

IV. On Reflection

In this report thus far, the crucially relevant point made, is that there are two systemic, and ultimately deadly, practical implications in the effect of a practiced doctrine which asserts that a competent physical science can be determined as a product of mathematics itself. One name for this delusion of the mathematicians is monetarism. However, varieties of this type of delusion of those mathematicians, such as the followers of the late Bertrand Russell, who took over the Solvay Conference proceedings of the 1920s, have misled dupes of this doctrine of so-called "Cambridge systems analysis" into delusions such as the cult of the International Institute for Applied Systems Analysis (IIASA), in which the plausibly dead walk silently forward, without ever actually moving.

The crucially relevant point made in this present report, is that there are two systemic, and ultimately deadly, practical implications of the effect of a practiced doctrine of merely mathematical notion of a system of mere money, such as what is termed "monetarism" today. This notion of mere money is to be contrasted with the notion of a system of credit, a notion of credit which is properly rooted in the notion of a general increase of physical-economically expressed anti-entropy in the power of mankind to increase the power expressed as anti-entropic progress of an increasing population to a higher physical and intellectual state of existence.

First: That the notion of money is intrinsically contrary to the inherently anti-entropic requirement for the organization of a durably successful form of growing physical economy.

Second: That, conversely, the simply arithmetically linear notion of money as such, is antithetical to the es-

sentially anti-entropic principle of Riemannian physical-economic progress. The quality of purchasing power for human benefit must become ever cheaper in terms of a nation's currency, but, that at the same time that the energy-flux density of the power employed is rising in a way which makes that power itself cheaper to the individual person. This accomplishment has already required progress to ever higher degrees of energy-flux density in terms of all relevant parameters of production and consumption.

So, monetary systems used as measures of value, as such, are inherently entropic, physically, in their effects. Thus, all economies which are ordered according to a notion of money as an intrinsic value, are implicitly doomed to decadence and ultimate self-destruction in one sense or another: unless, and until they might change their ways appropriately.

The roots of that problem of monetarism, and also monetarist tendencies, must be carefully examined, since the deeply embedded roots of the presently catastrophic world economic crisis must be traced to its origins in this aspect of the history of economy. The already referenced clinical case of Sumer is, therefore, an excellent choice of referents for the needed deeper insights into this matter, still today.

When Mathematics Is a Disease

Review and recast the relevant points which we have considered as bearing on that condemnation of monetarism, as follows.

As I have already indicated, the worst of the systemic crimes which ancient Mediterranean and medieval and modern European cultures have contributed as causes for the great, critical afflictions of society, that still today, were the subject of a great trilogy composed by the extraordinary genius of the ancient Aeschylus, the *Prometheus* trilogy. Long before the work of the disgusting Aristotle, Aeschylus had emphasized that the principle of evil in society was most clearly, most systemically shown in Aeschylus' own depiction of the "green evil" attributed to the quasi-fictive rule by the Olympian Zeus, the evil of a ban on mortal man's access to the knowledgeable use of "fire."

Instead of the symbolic quality of "fire," use today's better, real-life term: "energy-flux density." Nonetheless, it is the notable distinction of man from beast, that only people use fire.

The same notion attributed to that Olympian Zeus turns up in a certain specific way as the dogma of Aristotle. Two features of Aristotle's work cast relevant attention to the motive of Aristotle's crimes on this account. The two features express a common single principle.

In what I choose to point out first, we have the effect of Aristotle's influence on the work attributed to the geometer Euclid. In the second case, we have the Aristotelean assertion attributed to Friedrich Nietzsche, that "God is dead": the assertion that once the universe had been created, God Himself could never bring about any change in it; for Aristotle, God was no longer a Creator for such folk. Hence, for quasi-Aristotelean and rabid Dionysian Friedrich Nietzsche, God was already "dead." Nietzscheans Sombart, Schumpeter, and Larry Summers, have called it "creative destruction." Sometimes it is known by another name, "fascism."

In scrutinizing this pair of complementary examples of Aristotle and Euclid, we are being confronted by the greatest of all evils menacing the well-being of mankind today.

As I have already emphasized, this Aristotelean dogma also permeates the doctrine of the followers of Paolo Sarpi. Sarpi is sly in his own way, the way of the Satanism of the Venetian tribes.

Sarpi teaches his dupes to believe that they could not possibly know anything about the real universe. Adam Smith copies Sarpi on this point, exactly, in his *Theory of Moral Sentiments*. For Smith, man knows only the experience of pleasure and pain, of perceived rewards and punishment. For the British Liberals who follow Sarpi, there is no truth known to the believers, whereas the great arch-swindler and pure charlatan Sarpi himself, makes clear that he knows exactly what he is doing to a universality of mankind on his own account. To rule mankind, he is arguing, you must degrade people into becoming like a certain truly British type, either a slavering, lust-sodden beast, or a sly poisoner, like Sarpi's rival Aristotle, who practices religion within a peculiar sort of relic of a church where a baboon in a fancy ladies' dress presides at the services (although we have no present evidence that former Prime Minister Tony Blair ever presided in such services).

Writing on background about Sarpi's following, once we recognize that Sarpi wrote his doctrine for the proverbial suckers, not for himself, we need have no more illusion about Sarpi himself. The entirety of the doctrine he preached to such among his agents as Galileo, was, for him, one big lie, intended for no other purpose as much as to gull the proverbial dupes. His per-

sonal intention, and the method of his entire doctrine, was to effect destruction, that with a Satanic leer and manner of scheming. When we are engaged in treating the doctrine he preached to his British and other converts, we might think of a famous movie based upon a Sinclair Lewis novel, *Elmer Gantry*, which featured an insightful performance by actor Burt Lancaster and a stellar representation by another actor performing a most credible representation of a church-going "speaker in tongues."

For the part chosen to be played by the dupes of the charlatan Sarpi, read Adam Smith's confession in his 1759 *Theory of the Moral Sentiments*. It is the effect on nations and peoples of the doctrine created by Sarpi for the credulities of the dupes, which is the subject which I address here, as follows.

Where Smith wrote, in his 1759 "Theory:" "…Nature has directed us …," Sarpi's intention was to think, "Satan has directed them." Read the relevant passage from the 1759 work which I have frequently cited, in the following, slightly altered way:

"Satan has directed us … by original and immediate instincts. Hunger, thirst, the passion which unites the two sexes, the love of pleasure, and the dread of pain, prompt us to apply those means for their own sakes, and without any consideration of their tendency to those beneficent ends which the great Director of nature [Satan] intended to produce by them."

Smith is a dutifully credulous slave of the intention which a gloating Satan wields, the temptation of foolish men and women to become accomplices or instruments of their own destruction.

That said, now read Aeschylus' *Prometheus* to the following effect, as I have spoken of this matter earlier.

Certain people of the sea, having accomplished the murder of their father on behalf of their mother, Olympia, or perhaps a synonym for "the Whore of Babylon," came to call themselves "gods," and, to lord this adopted authority over what were treated as the virtual slaves called ordinary men and women. Such self-styled "gods," constituted the immortal body of the inhabitants of the imperial court of the Olympian Zeus who reigned in the memory of his mother, Olympia.

It was on behalf of the court of those so-called "gods" that the companions of Zeus tormented the merely mortal gladiators of the arena. See that Paolo Sarpi casting himself in the role of that Olympian Zeus. Read the part written for the character Iago in the revised, second edition of Giuseppe Verdi's *Otello*: "I believe in a cruel god." Cast that monologue played by Iago as an incarnation of Satan, and you have a fair replica of the self-image of that would-be Satan who is known as Paolo Sarpi. There you have the essence of what is called "British Liberalism." There, you should also recognize the role of the "Executioner" under the Terror of the Spanish Inquisition and the French Revolution. Like the Satanic Torquemada, the principle of "the terror," which is Sarpi's part in real life, is "If I could be God, I would prefer to be Satan."

There, in that role of the Iago of the soliloquy, you have the model for the figures of the World Wildlife Fund's Princes Philip and Bernhard. When you begin to see the real-life Paolo Sarpi and his works in that way, you have understood the moving spirit of the present British imperial system and its most powerful flunkeys, its leading bankers. It is those who fail to grasp the notion of Sarpi as a Satanic model made in the fashion of his own adopted sense of identity, who have yet to understand the essence of the British imperial system. You have only to ask the tormented victims of the British role in Africa. Read the flunkey Adam Smith with the actually Satanic figure of Sarpi in mind. See Sarpi, not Smith! Or, see the Abbé Antonio S. Conti who adopted the Eighteenth-century British mission of destroying science in the name of the silly puppet of a "black magic fantasist" known as Isaac Newton.

That is the true intention expressed in the preferred, and very silly, British subject's use of the term "human nature." Think of Oscar Wilde's casting of "The Picture of Dorian Gray."

Think of the schemers who orchestrated Gray's self-destruction: How very, very British!

There is a crucial sort of importance, for almost any citizen, in viewing that Sarpian page from the book of British imperial ideology as I have just summarized the case of Sarpi here. What is the alternative to the practice of that self-degradation fairly identified as contemporary "British ideology"? British man and woman crafted according to the social recipes of British ideology, have no actual sense of immortality, since that type spends its mortal years to the effect of one who has adopted the life's mission of digging its own grave, wearing a first- or second-class tombstone, or even none at all, as its destiny. Such "Brits" have no true sense of immortality, no sense of mankind's immortal mission in having lived in his or her own life's time.

The truly creative human personality is not of that wretched type, a fact which I, personally, richly enjoy. What are the true fruits of the tree of a certain immortality to be enjoyed in the course of living?

The Secret of Life

Putting it in figurative terms of reference, what is the death of a human individual? Or, better said, what is a valid sense of immortality? Let us name the answer to such questions as an efficiently practiced principle of "immortality."

Take the case of Christopher Columbus who adopted the mission handed to him by circles of the then-deceased Cardinal Nicholas of Cusa. Cusa, after recognizing the systemic corruption still reigning in the Europe and Asia known to him in his time, informed his associates of the mission of crossing the great oceans to other continents, to develop a culture which would produce the remedy needed for the corruption dominating the contemporary cultures of the already known world.

In that sense, Cusa was thus already living in the future of humanity: a future state of civilization.

There are principally two ways of viewing such intentions. One is the notion of success in reaching a new place, one better suited to one's intention for making improvements in the presently experienced kind of human condition. The other view, is that of improving the immortal quality of the existence of the universe itself. That latter view is associated with the notion of the role of human creativity expressed by producing better systemic states of nature than exist presently. That latter choice stated otherwise, we are presently pointing in the direction of states of human existence of a better quality than are known to us now. That latter choice, considered as a type, corresponds to the effect of the discovery of a new, higher universal principle. The true alternative to the trash represented by such as Paolo Sarpi.

This set of notions has a notable contemporary expression in the set of scientific achievements of the Academician V.I. Vernadsky's development of the principled notions of the distinctions of, and functional interdependency among what are presently named the Lithosphere, Biosphere, and Noösphere. The result of the scientific elaboration of the development of that set of notions, confronts us with the reality of an anti-entropic order in the universe, which is a rejection of that great lie which the Gods of Olympus have taught those victims identified as hopelessly mortal, ordinary men and women.

To say it otherwise, and that is necessary, true human beings live to create an improved future state of the universe. In other words, we must order our lives in the direction of changes which Albert Einstein's view of truly anti-entropic, universal relativity implies. This is realized, in practice, by devoting one's life to bringing such a future state into being.

We have recently revived what had been the mission of building an improved state of organization of our continent which had been known as "North American Water and Power Alliance (NAWAPA)." The design of that clearly feasible accomplishment had been prompted by the success of President Franklin Roosevelt's magnificent success in the transformation of a major portion of the territory of the United States, "The Tennessee Valley Authority (TVA)." However, as we reflect on that history since the TVA itself was begun in 1933, NAWAPA is not only an enormous undertaking relative to the TVA; the difference is qualitative in effect. The realization of NAWAPA changes the quality of existence of our planet, and reaches out to the prospect of changes within our Solar System as well.

The prospect of mankind residing within the Solar System, beckons our attention to the relativistic prospects for the galaxy, and beyond. Instead of man as a poor serf of a same-same world, we are now man creating future states of human existence on, and also beyond this planet. We are considering, thus, an effort which is comparable to, but supersedes, the mission assigned by Cardinal Nicholas of Cusa, and implemented in part by a Christopher Columbus inspired by the work of Cusa. Man may achieve effective immortality by creating the future, higher state of society which has been produced by aid of his existence.

This is the business of creating the future, higher quality of states of existence, through discovery of what a rigorous practice of scientific progress recognizes as the anti-entropic process of applied discovery of newly discovered universal physical principles. Rather than merely acquiring and inhabiting a place in which to live (and die), we are creating new places, even new planets, and beyond, in which to live.

This quality of progress requires the discovery of new physical and comparable principles which are

EIRNS/Stuart Lewis

Lyndon LaRouche: "Man may achieve effective immortality by creating the future, higher state of society which has been produced by aid of his existence."

products created by the noetic powers specific to the mind of the individual member of the human species, which represents a certain kind of participation in immortality. This, in itself, is a practice which creates a general state of human existence, in which man is no longer essentially mortal. The products of true creation are immortal in and of themselves; they remain a living part of the universe when our celebrated "mortal coil" has passed.

There is a principle involved in all this. To be immortal, contribute to creating specifically immortal results, and the real you will never have died. Such has been the intention expressed, as to matters of principle, in Moses Mendelssohn's reading of Plato's ***Phaedo*** (***Phaedon***).

The Matter of Mental States

In a matter of reflection on the preceding content of this present report as a whole, the crucial point in this present writing as a whole, is my repeated emphasis on the distinction of a notion of mankind as defined by mere powers of sense-perception, from the quite different quality of a personal identity which is located as the identity of the person who owns the tools which are the given powers of sense-perception delivered as part of the auxiliary material that "comes with, and in the box."

Such is the distinction of the fully realized human personality expressed by the willful consciousness of creative powers, from the type associated with the poor serf who must do as his father and grandfather did when cast into the sensory state of political brutality by the non-gods of the Olympian Zeus' system of imperial reign.

Our experience with the category of studies associated with the notion of the "physical tensor," as has been shown for the case of replicating the actual method employed by Carl F. Gauss in his actual discovery of the orbit of the asteroid Ceres, should remind us that there is no ready-made sort of mathematics from which the physical order of development within our universe might be deduced. Rather, the fact is, as the case of the discoveries by Bernhard Riemann exemplify the relevant types of connections, that it is progress in the creative development of physical science, on which all valid improvements in mathematical applications depend. It is that notion of the existence of actual physical principles as such, as prior to an experimentally settled mathematics, which is the essential foundation of physical-scientific progress.

So, in this fashion, the role of that aspect of the human individual identity which is essential, and which the sundry instruments of sense-perception merely serve as the creative powers of that personal identity of individual human reason may demand.

We have come closer and closer to the conclusion, that we must put human sense-perception in its proper place, just as Albert Einstein did in adducing from Johannes Kepler's actual discovery of universal gravitation, that the universe to which Kepler's attention had been addressed, must be focused on the field of cosmic radiation which fills up the space represented by what poor sense-perceptual powers mistake, with silly sense-perception's mistaken egotism, as "empty." Einstein had read Kepler's achievement as coherent with a notion of universal physical space-time as being finite but unbounded. It is not only unbounded; it is growing, anti-entropically.

And, we are part of that.

On this account, I have frequently referred to the closing paragraphs of Percy Bysshe Shelley's *A Defence of Poetry,* where he emphasizes the evidence that in certain situations of mass behavior of large portions of populations, such as we noted such patterns of mass behavior in political assemblies which erupted suddenly during August 2009, there are faculties of communication which show themselves to have a very specific quality of existence during such times, and, yet,

would seem to possess no organ to be held accountable for such a uniquely remarkable expression as mass behavior.

Such exceptional instances of a quality of "mass behavior," are to be associated in a clinical way with the late William Empson's notion of a virtually physical principle of metaphorical irony in its most successful expression as such.

Such a paradoxical consideration should not surprise those among us who think carefully, and with well-focused concentration on relevant phenomena. The crucial fact about creativity, whether ostensibly scientific or Classical-artistic in expression, is that it is located, primarily, not in mathematics, but in the mental processes which are relatively more familiar to us from the domain of Classical-artistic creativity.

A notable case for consideration in examining such social phenomena, is the effect of the post-World War II role of a movement associated with the role of existentialism under the influence of The Congress for Cultural Freedom, and similar expressions of cultural-intellectual depravity experienced already during the period of the post-World War I 1920s. The "de-Classicalization" of the performance of Classical music defined by its foundations within the domain of the work of Johann Sebastian Bach, in the form of Romanticism applied even to the performance of the work of specifically Classical composers in the continued Bach tradition, is correlated with similar waning of actual mental-productive creativity among the end-products of university education. The loss of the role of metaphor is a most crucial social phenomenon on this account.

Or, to restate the same point, in a necessary, alternate fashion, insight into such issues on the fringes of science as it is defined today, will find their solutions in the process of clarifying the distinctions between the notion of self, rooted in sense-perception as such, and the notion of the human creative-mental identity which uses sense-perceptual powers as merely auxiliaries attached to those creative powers of the human mind which are the actual seat of the inner human sense of functions of personal identity. This qualifying view of the limitations of sense-perception as such, tends to open the mind of the person's inner identity, to bring attention to forms of communication, perhaps within the domain of cosmic radiation, which may betray themselves as being the equivalent of "additional qualities of potential sense-perception," as in the domain of Classical artistic metaphor.